SERVING ONE ANOTHER

GENE A. GETZ

This book is designed for your personal reading pleasure and profit. It is also designed for group study. A leader's guide with helps and hints for teachers and visual aids (Victor Multiuse Transparency Masters) is available from your local bookstore or from the publisher.

VICTOR BOOKS® a division of SP Publications, Inc.
WHEATON, ILLINOIS 60187

Offices also in
Whitby, Ontario, Canada
Amersham-on-the-Hill, Bucks, England

Other books by Gene Getz:
Building Up One Another
Loving One Another
Encouraging One Another
Praying for One Another

Unless otherwise noted, Scripture quotations are taken from the *Holy Bible: New International Version,* © 1978 by the New York International Bible Society. Used by permission of Zondervan Bible Publishers. Other quotations are from the *King James Version* (KJV) and from the *New American Standard Bible* (NASB), © the Lockman Foundation 1960, 1962, 1963, 1968, 1971, 1972, 1973, 1975, 1977. Used by permission.

Recommended Dewey Decimal Classification: 248.4
Suggested Subject Heading: CHRISTIAN LIFE

Library of Congress Catalog Card Number: 83-51311
ISBN: 0-88207-612-4

Printed in the United States of America

VICTOR BOOKS
A division of SP Publications, Inc.
Wheaton, Illinois 60187

Contents

Why This Study?

No concept is more significant in bringing renewal to a local church than that of "serving." It is at the heart of meaningful Christian relationships—whether in the church at large, in the family (the church in miniature), or in the relationship between husband and wife. A servant spirit is also foundational to an effective witness in the world. If "loving one another" is foundational in being able to practice the "one another" concepts specified in Scripture, then "serving one another" is the most comprehensive manifestation of that foundational concept.

Renewal—A Biblical Perspective

Renewal is the essence of dynamic Christianity and the basis on which Christians, both in a corporate or "body" sense and as individual believers, can determine the will of God. Paul made this clear when he wrote to the Roman Christians—"be transformed by the *renewing of your mind.* Then," he continued, "you will be able to test and approve what God's will is" (Rom. 12:2). Here Paul is talking about renewal in a corporate sense. In other words, Paul is asking these Christians as a *body* of believers, to develop the mind of Christ through corporate renewal.

Personal renewal will not happen as God intended it unless it happens in the context of corporate renewal. On the other hand, corporate renewal will not happen as God intended without personal renewal. Both are necessary.

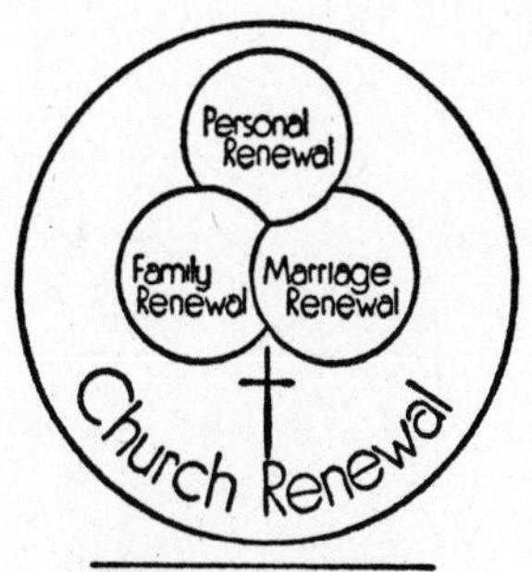

Biblical Renewal

Developing the mind of Christ

The larger circle represents "church renewal." This is the most comprehensive concept in the New Testament. However, every local church is made up of smaller self-contained, but interrelated units. The *family* in Scripture emerges as the "church in miniature." In turn, the family is made up of an even smaller social unit—*marriage.* The third inner circle represents *personal* renewal, which is inseparably linked to all of the other basic units. Marriage is made up of two separate individuals who become one. The family is made up of parents and children who are also to reflect the mind of Christ. And the church is made up of not only individual Christians, but couples and families.

Though all of these social units are interrelated, biblical renewal can begin within any specific social unit. But wherever it begins—in the church, families, marriages, or individuals—the process immediately touches all the other social units. And one thing is certain! All that God says is consistent and harmonious. He does not have one set of principles for the church and another set for the family, another for husbands and wives, and another for individual Christians. For example, the principles God outlines for local church elders, fathers, and husbands regarding their roles as leaders are interrelated and consistent. If they are not, we can be sure that we have not interpreted God's plan accurately.

Remember too that biblical renewal is not an end in itself.

The body of Christ is to build itself up in love so that the unity produced will serve as a bridge to reach a lost world for Jesus Christ—as individuals, as married couples, as a total family, and as a total church. This was the essence of Christ's prayer in John 17: "May they be brought to complete unity *to let the world know* that You sent Me and have loved them even as You have loved Me" (17:23).

Additional Studies in Biblical Renewal

The following books are part of the Biblical Renewal Series by Gene Getz designed to provide supportive help in moving toward renewal. They all fit into one of the circles described here and will provoke thought and provide interaction and tangible steps toward growth.

"ONE ANOTHER" SERIES	*PERSONALITY SERIES*	*THE "MEASURE OF" SERIES*
Building Up One Another	*Abraham*	*Measure of a . . .*
Encouraging One Another	*David*	*Church*
Loving One Another	*Joseph*	*Family*
Praying for One Another	*Joshua*	*Man*
	Moses	*Marriage*
	Nehemiah	*Woman*
	Elijah	*Christian—Philippians*
		Christian—Titus
		Christian—James 1

Sharpening the Focus of the Church presents an overall perspective for Church Renewal. All of these books are available from your Christian bookstore.

My wife Elaine and I affectionately dedicate this volume to our good friends and neighbors, Herb and Anne Stem, who in a very special way exemplify the theme of this book.

They are servants extraordinary. Their love for Christ and others is constant and practical. More than they know, they have encouraged us with their servant hearts—not only in their ministry to us personally, but as we have seen them continually reach out to others.

Thank you, Herb and Anne, for serving us—and others—in love!

1

Serve One Another in Love

A budding artist once painted a picture of the Last Supper. He took it to the writer Leo Tolstoy for his opinion. Carefully and understandingly, the Russian master of words studied the canvas. Then pointing to the central figure, he declared, "You do not love Him."

"Why, that is the Lord Jesus Christ," exclaimed the artist.

"I know," insisted Tolstoy, "but you do not love Him. If you loved Him more, you would paint Him better."

Few of us are budding artists in this sense, but the Bible teaches we're all to be *servants*—servants of the Lord Jesus Christ and one another. With this in mind, we can easily reword Tolstoy's statement to read, "If you loved Him more, you would serve Him better." And the next step, particularly in view of our subject, is to reword the statement even further: "If we loved *one another more,* we would *serve one another* better." Thus Paul wrote to the Galatians, "You, my brothers, were called to be free. But do not use your freedom to indulge the sinful nature; rather, *serve one another in love*" (Gal. 5:13).*

We Are to Be Servants

In Galatians 5:13 Paul teaches us that we are to *serve.* There are four basic words in the language of the New Testament that are often translated "serve," "servant," or "serving." All in all, this basic concept is used over 300 times in the New Testament (about 130 times in the Gospels and Acts and approximately 170 times in the Epistles).

The two words that are used more frequently are *douleō* and *diakoneō*. *Douleō* literally means to be a slave; to serve; to obey; to submit to. New Testament writers used this word both in a good and a bad sense. On the positive side, the word means to serve God and others in a context of Christian love. On the negative side, *douleō* means to become a slave to some base power. For example, in Paul's letter to the Romans he taught that people can be "slaves to sin" (Rom. 6:6).

Diakoneō means to *minister* to someone. In a more specific sense, New Testament writers used this word to describe someone who serves people food and drink; someone who cares for others' material needs. In a more general sense, it describes those who attend to *anything* that may serve another's interest. It is from this concept that we get the word *deacon.*

It is clear from these definitions that the first word, *douleō,* is the stronger in meaning. A *doulos* was a slave, a bondman, a person of servile conditions. In its strongest

---

*Hereafter, all italicized words in Scripture references are for author's emphasis.

sense, this word described a person who gave himself up completely to another's will. This concept is used most frequently in the New Testament (approximately 160 times). And this is the concept that Paul used when he wrote, "*Serve* one another in love" (Gal. 5:13). He was writing about serving one another in the most devoted sense. As believers, we are to give ourselves totally to one another—to literally become slaves to one another.

What a contrast to the emphasis in modern society! Look at the newsstands and survey the titles of current magazines that focus on "me" and "myself." The thrust of these publications are that *I* am important; *my* rights are what are the most significant thing. If my rights conflict with your rights, *I* come first. If you cannot meet my needs and I cannot meet your needs—if we can't work it out together—you go your way and I'll go mine.

In his book *Improving Your Serve,* Chuck Swindoll identifies this emphasis with a verbal pyramid. At the top is "I," moving down to "me," "mine," and "myself" (Word Books, p. 28).

I
M E
M I N E
M Y S E L F

Why this emphasis? For one thing, it is a reaction against a perversion of the concept of submission, particularly as it relates to women and their relationship to men. In fact, most modern magazines that deal with freedom focus on the rights of women. This focus reflects a reaction against male dominance and control that has permeated world history.

However, this new emphasis on freedom to be oneself, to

do one's own thing, points to a more basic problem. It reflects the sin principle that is active in us all. Ever since Adam and Eve disobeyed God, all of mankind has become self-oriented. Men have become dominant and often cruel, not only in their attitudes and actions toward women, but toward all other human beings. Women have often become selfish, unsubmissive, and resistant to any form of authority. True, much of this tendency is a reaction against male dominance and selfishness, but in its roots it is also a reflection of the sin principle that is active in us all. Left to myself, I concentrate on myself—*my* rights, *my* needs, *my* interests. This is my natural bent. And so it is with all mankind—men *and* women.

What then is the solution to this problem? In context, the Apostle Paul answers that question.

We Are to Serve One Another

Jesus Christ made it possible for all of us to break out of our self-oriented mold. In Christ we are set free to minister to others, to love others as ourselves (Gal. 5:14). When we become Christians we are given new life—eternal life—and with that great gift we are given the potential and the power to get beyond ourselves and experience the fulfillment that comes to those who serve others. This is what Jesus Christ meant when He said, "For whoever wants to save his life will lose it, but whoever loses his life for Me will find it" (Matt. 16:25).

Christianity is *relational*. First, it involves a personal relationship with Jesus Christ. We become Christians, not just by acknowledging that Jesus Christ is the Son of God, but by *receiving* Him as our personal Lord and Saviour. John wrote that "to all who *received* Him, to those who *believed* in His name, He gave the right to become children of God" (John 1:12). And when we receive Jesus Christ in this sense, we have a unique *relationship with Him.*

But a new relationship in Christ and with Christ is more than *vertical.* It is also *horizontal.* We become members of Christ's body, the church. By one Spirit we are all placed into one body (1 Cor. 12:13). Just as there are many interrelated and coordinated members in a human body, so it is within Christ's body. Each of us is related to all other parts of that body (v. 26).

The New Testament word *allélôn,* which is most frequently translated "one another," is used over 60 times in the New Testament to describe how we as Christians are to function in a corporate sense. (See *Building Up One Another,* also by Gene Getz and published by Victor. This book develops the "one another" concepts as they appear in the New Testament.) Furthermore, there are numerous other words that describe this same process. Christianity is indeed *relational.* This is why Paul instructed the Galatians to "serve *one another.*"

This process, however, must be guided by a divine principle. This leads to the third concept in Paul's directive.

We Are to Serve One Another in Love

Paul told the Galatian Christians they were "called to be free." However, they were not to use that "freedom to indulge the sinful nature" (Gal. 5:13a). In other words, it is possible to serve others in an inappropriate and carnal way.

What should guide us in our relationships with others? We are, Paul wrote, to "serve one another *in love.*" To make the point even clearer, he reminded the Galatians that "the entire law is summed up in a single command: '*Love* your neighbor as yourself' "(v. 14).

The two basic words for love used in the New Testament *(agapaō* and *phileō)* are used over 300 times. Almost exactly half the times this concept is used to refer to our relationship with God and the other half to our relationship with one another. This is very significant in view of Christ's answer to the Pharisees when asked, "Which is the greatest commandment?" Jesus answered: " '*Love the Lord your God* with all your heart and with all your soul and with all your mind.' This is the first and greatest commandment. And the second is like it: '*Love your neighbor* as yourself.' All the law and the prophets hang on these two commandments" (Matt. 22:36-40).

Other New Testament writers verify that love is the divine principle that should guide us in our relationships. John, particularly, emphasized this point. In his first epistle, he used the word *love* nearly 50 times. Five times he expressly wrote, "Love one another" (1 John 3:11, 23; 4:7, 11, 12).

The Apostle Paul again and again demonstrated in his letters that love is the most important criterion in measuring the quality of Christian relationships. Note the following statements:

- And now these three remain: faith, hope, and *love*. But the greatest of these is *love* (1 Cor. 13:13).
- Follow the way of *love* (14:1).
- Do everything in *love* (16:14).
- Be patient, bearing with one another in *love* (Eph. 4:2).

- Speaking the truth in *love* (4:15).
- Live a life of *love,* just as Christ *loved* us and gave Himself up for us (5:2).
- And over all these virtues put on *love* (Col. 3:14).
- Pursue... *love* (2 Tim. 2:22).

Love, as it is defined in Scripture, is the guiding principle in all Christian relationships, including the process of *serving one another.* Without Christlike love, our relationships can be dominated by selfishness and painful bondage. Serving others becomes a negative experience rather than a positive one. But guided by the divine principle of love, serving others becomes a powerful demonstration of corporate Christlikeness.

Determining My Serving Quotient

Every Christian needs to pause periodically and ask this question: To what extent am I serving others in love? This question, of course, breaks down into several sub-questions.

1. To what extent are others in the body of Christ serving me without my serving them?

Some Christians receive and receive, but never give anything in return. Don't misunderstand. I'm not talking exclusively about money. Certainly that is a factor, but there are some who say, "I'll give anything! Just don't ask for my money!"

However, there are many other factors involved in serving. There are Christians who:

- Have received the Gospel freely, but never share it with anyone else.
- Learn the Word of God regularly, but never teach

it to others.

- Let other Christians minister to their own children, but never minister to other Christians' children.
- Receive compliments, but never compliment others.
- Wait for people to reach out to them, but never reach out to others.
- Receive gifts of love from others, but never share gifts of love in return.
- Receive notes of appreciation, but never write notes themselves.

There are many ways to evaluate our service to others. Do you identify with any of the preceding statements?

2. To what extent do others in my immediate family serve me without my serving in return?

HUSBAND-WIFE RELATIONSHIPS. There are husbands and wives who receive and receive from their spouses, but give very little in return. In fact, they very seldom say "thank you."

There are husbands who say, "I work hard all day; I put bread on the table; I provide for her. What more does she want?" The answer is that she wants "you"—your sensitivity, your understanding, your listening ear, your tenderness.

There are wives who say, "I cook the meals; wash the clothes; care for the kids. What more does he want?" The answer is that he wants "you"—your sympathetic ear, your warm touch, the twinkle in your eye—and, yes, all the things you want from him.

A scene between Tevye and Goldie from *Fiddler on the Roof* illustrates these points. Their world of security, held together by their traditions, was crumbling around them as their daughters one by one "fell in love" and then married outside of their Jewish culture. In the Jewish community in which they lived in Russia, it just didn't happen that way. Your mate was predetermined by your parents and hopefully you would learn to love one another after you were married.

On one occasion, Tevye turned to Goldie, his wife of 25 years, and asked her if she loved him. Goldie avoided the question as long as she could. Then she named all the chores she'd done for her husband over the years. But Tevye still wanted to know if she loved him. Finally, Goldie reminded him that they had lived together, fought together, and starved together for 25 years. If that didn't prove her love, what would? (Charles Hansen Music and Books, Inc., pp. 40-43)

The point of application of this exchange is that sometimes we serve another, not in love, but out of duty and a sense of responsibility and obligation. When that happens, "serving" becomes a negative experience rather than a positive one as God intended.

PARENT-CHILD RELATIONSHIPS. There are children who take their parents for granted—receiving, but never giving.

There are parents who take their children for granted—never rewarding them for their responsiveness and co-operation.

I remember when our grown daughters were very small, Elaine and I used to travel from our home in Wheaton, Illinois to Schroon Lake, New York to minister in a youth camp. As we drove across the country, our two little girls would play for hours in the backseat, contented as could be. My wife was very wise in providing them with "little girl" projects to keep them occupied. However, after several hours, they would get fidgety, lose interest in what they were doing, and begin to "pick" at each other. My response was to warn them several times, and when they continued to fuss at each other, I would then send them to their respective "corners" in the backseat of the car.

One day my wife reminded me that for hours they were content and I seemed to never notice. But when they finally got bored and tired and began to create problems, then I noticed. In other words, I was "rewarding them negatively" when they got irritable and fussy, but never "rewarding them positively" when they were content and happy.

That experience taught me a lesson. How often do we reward our children in this way, but take their good behavior for granted?

In many respects, the family is oftentimes the most difficult place to serve others. We find ourselves gladly helping those outside of our families, but neglecting those closest to us.

I'm amazed at how often I find myself being tested and tempted in the very areas of scriptural truths I'm researching and teaching others. It seems God allows me to experience my own level of maturity (or immaturity) in the specific realms of Christian living I'm trying to communicate to others. And often I find myself discovering my own weaknesses and inability to measure up. It is the same with the concept of serving. When I was writing this chapter on serving one another in love, my wife shared something with me I needed to hear, but I reacted very negatively and defensively. Rather than approaching the idea with a servant's heart, I responded in an inappropriate way.

What a conflict I generated in my soul! My sense of freedom in preparation was totally gone. There was no way I could continue preparing material on "serving" until I faced my own failure to practice this concept. To restore this freedom actually meant getting my eyes off myself, getting them on others, and asking forgiveness of my wife for reacting the way I did.

Has this ever happened to you? God knows our areas of weakness. And so does Satan. Somehow, the Lord in His sovereign way can even turn temptation and failure into a lesson in Christian growth—if we'll let Him!

Setting a Goal

Look back over the applicational section of this chapter ("Determining My Serving Quotient"). Select *one area* where you feel you can more effectively serve another Christian in love. It may be in your family. It may be in your church. It may be with those you work with on the job. It may be within your circle of close friends.

This week I will: ______________________________

____

____

2
Freedom to Serve

I never cease to be amazed when I board a huge jumbo jet and experience firsthand the law of aerodynamics at work. For example, the huge Boeing 747 seats up to 500 passengers and when fully loaded with people, luggage, and fuel it weighs up to 400 tons. When ready for takeoff the crew activates four huge jet engines. The thrust is so powerful you can actually feel yourself pushed back against your seat. Less than a minute later, that huge machine that measures nearly the distance of a football field is airborne, climbing skyward to a normal altitude of nearly 40,000 feet and traveling nearly 600 miles an hour. People who travel a great deal take this experience for granted, but can you imagine what Orville and Wilbur Wright would have thought and felt if they could have been a part of this incredible phenomenon? They would probably have been candidates for cardiac arrest!

What is so amazing is that the law of gravity dictates that

something so huge and so heavy should never get off the ground. In fact, I am six feet tall and weigh about 180 pounds. Yet, I have never been able to jump high enough to dunk a basketball in a 10-foot hoop. To be able to do so, I would have to overcome the law of gravity.

This explains why a 747 weighing so much can lift off a runway and soar like an eagle. Its powerful jet engines and engineering design defy the law of gravity. In this instance, the law of aerodynamics at work through human ingenuity is more powerful than the law of gravity.

This principle is also true in the spiritual realm. The Bible talks about the "law of sin and death" that is active in every human being who has ever lived (Rom. 8:2). But the Scriptures also reveal a law that is greater and more powerful and which can be activated, not by human engineering, but by God Himself. It is the "law of the Spirit of life" that was made available by the coming of Jesus Christ (v. 2). It is this law that sets us free to serve God and others in love. This is why Paul discusses serving in the context of freedom. If we are not "free in Christ," we cannot be "free to serve" as God intended. Paul wrote, "You, my brothers, were called to be *free*. But do not use your *freedom* to indulge the sinful nature; rather, serve one another in love" (Gal. 5:13).

Freedom in Christ: Available through Faith

Paul begins this section of his letter with a statement on freedom. However, he had already introduced this concept when he wrote, "It is for *freedom* that Christ has set us *free*" (5:1).

To understand this wonderful spiritual reality more fully, we must look at another letter Paul wrote, his epistle to the

Romans. After culminating a very intriguing section of Scripture dealing with the conflict that often exists between a Christian's old and new natures, Paul concluded, "Therefore, there is now no condemnation for those who are in Christ Jesus, because through Christ Jesus [here he refers to the greater law] the *law of the Spirit of life* set me *free* from the *law of sin and death*" (Rom. 8:1-2).

Before conversion to Christ, all people were "*slaves* to sin" (6:16). Here Paul uses *doulos* to describe a person who was a slave. As we've noted, this is the strongest concept for "serving" used in the New Testament. In its most intense sense, it refers to being in bondage to another person. Thus, it is a very appropriate word, for in our unconverted state we were "*slaves* to sin." We were in *bondage.* In the Galatian letter, Paul illustrates this point by saying we were in *prison,* "locked up until faith should be revealed" (Gal. 3:23).

After conversion to Christ, Paul states that we "have been set *free* from sin and have become *slaves* to righteousness" (Rom. 6:18). Though this may sound contradictory—that is, to be a "slave" and yet "free"—in reality there is only one way to be truly free and that is to conform our lives to the will of God. To experience life as God intended it, we must live in harmony with our Creator.

Freedom is a very misunderstood word. There are those who talk about being free from parents, free from social restrictions, free from the influence of other authority figures—or just free from other people's involvement in our lives. To a certain extent, we may experience that kind of freedom. And to a certain extent, we *need* to experience that kind of freedom. As human beings we're entitled to a certain amount of "space."

However, there is an area in which we will never be free unless we accept God's offer of salvation. We will always be slaves to sin. Furthermore, since we are social creatures, we will never be free from the influence of sin as it manifests itself through the lives of others.

But there is a solution to this problem. Jesus Christ has come to set us free. He said, "I tell you the truth, everyone who sins is a *slave to sin*" (John 8:34). But Jesus had already said, "If you hold to My teaching, you are really My disciples. Then you will know the *truth,* and the *truth will set you free*" (vv. 31-32).

In essence, what is the truth Jesus Christ is talking about? Later He answered that question when He said, "I am . . . the truth. . . . No one comes to the Father except through Me" (14:6).

Jesus Christ is our source of freedom. And the Scriptures make it clear that this freedom in Christ is *available through faith.* "Therefore, since we have been justified *through faith,* we have peace with God through our Lord Jesus Christ, through whom we have gained access *by faith* into this grace in which we now stand" (Rom. 5:1-2).

At this point, we should note that we are not free to do what *we* want to do, but free to walk in God's will. In fact, true freedom comes when what God desires is what we desire. What greater freedom is there than to be in harmony with the Creator of the universe? In fact, there is no other way to be free. All other avenues that appear to give freedom are illusions that will ultimately lead to heartache and disappointment. The subtle part is that what we choose to do may "feel good" and "seem fulfilling" at the moment. But in the end, attitudes and actions that violate the will of God ultimately lead to disillusionment, and in some instances, great tragedy.

Freedom in Christ—Appropriated by Acceptance

When is a Christian free? The Bible teaches that as believers we "*have* been set free from sin" the moment we truly put our faith in Christ (Rom. 6:18, 22). When we become Christians, sin is no longer our master (v. 14). When by faith we trust Christ as our Saviour, we identify with His death. In the process, we actually die with Christ. Paul writes that "our old self [old nature] was crucified with Him so that the body of sin might be rendered powerless, that we should no longer be slaves to sin" (v. 6). Paul states further that "anyone who has died has been *freed* from sin" (v. 7).

This doctrinal truth often poses a problem for Christians. "What do you mean, I've been freed from sin?" they ask. "I still sin. I still fail God. I still do things I shouldn't do. I say things I shouldn't say. I think things I shouldn't think. I've acted selfishly. I've even been immoral and unethical. I've been impatient and unkind. Yet, I know that I'm a Christian. I have put my faith in Christ. Why am I not free from sin?"

Nowhere does the Bible teach that we are "free from sin" in the sense that we will no longer be tempted to sin, or that we will never sin, or that we do not have freedom to sin. That is why Paul warned the Galatians not to use their freedom in Christ "to indulge the sinful nature" (Gal. 5:13).

What the Bible is teaching is that we are free from the *power* of sin. We don't have to serve sin and the old nature. The prison door is open. All we have to do is walk out into a new world of freedom and new life.

When Corrie ten Boom was given notice that she was

going to be released from a Nazi prison camp, she was led to the courtyard and from there to the prison gates. Later she wrote:

> The gate swung open and I glimpsed the lake in front of the camp. I could smell freedom.
>
> "Follow me," a young girl in an officer's uniform said to me. I walked slowly through the gate, never looking back. Behind me I heard the hinges squeak as the gate swung shut. I was free, and flooding through my mind were the words of Jesus to the church of Philadelphia: "Behold, I have set before thee an open door, and no man can shut it" (Rev. 3:8, KJV. From *Tramp for the Lord*, Fleming H. Revell Co., p. 24).

If Corrie had not *accepted* the fact she was free and had returned to her dormitory rather than walking through the gate, she would have chosen to stay in prison rather than accept her freedom. Theoretically she would have still been free, but not experientially.

And so it is with many Christians. The prison door is open and we have been set free. Sin is no longer our master. But unfortunately, many Christians don't walk through the prison door and out into the sunlight of God's grace and love. We choose to stay in the wrong environment, the wrong place, associating with the wrong people. We do not appropriate our freedom—which leads to the next step to freedom.

Freedom in Christ—Activated by Obedience

The crew in a 747 can sit at the end of a runway all day long, *knowing* that the plane is *free* to take off. They may have received clearance from the tower again and again. They also know that the power is available. But the plane will never get off the ground unless the jet engines are activated. The plane must be in a moving position.

Just so with the Christian. I can *know* I am free in Christ. And I can *accept* that truth as a reality. But I will never live above this world's system without obeying God's doctrines and applying God's principles. It is the truth *applied* that really sets me free. Consequently, Paul wrote:

> Do not let sin reign in your mortal body so that you *obey* its evil desires. Do not offer the parts of your body to sin, as instruments of wickedness, but rather offer yourselves to God, as those who have been brought from death to life; and offer the parts of your body to Him as instruments of righteousness (Rom. 6:12-13).

Later Paul put it all together in several culminating statements:

> Therefore, I urge you, brothers, in view of God's mercy, *to offer your bodies as living sacrifices*, holy and pleasing to God—which is your spiritual worship. Do not conform any longer to the pattern of this world, but be transformed by the renewing of your mind. Then you will be able to test and approve what God's will is—His good, pleasing, and perfect will (12:1-2).

Nothing can compare with the freedom we experience when we walk in harmony with the Creator of the universe, conforming our lives to His will and desires. This does not mean we lose our individual personalities in some corporate entity or essence. This does not mean that we lose our self-identity. Rather, we are free to become all that God created us to become. Our self-identity is established. We are set free from ourselves—free to reach out, to give, to share—in short, we are free to serve God and one another. We truly lose our lives to find them again.

Obedience to the will of God is a *process*. True freedom in Christ is something that must be nurtured and developed. We must *renew our minds*. When we do not, we are headed for failure in our Christian lives.

I began this chapter with an illustration from the world of aviation. Let me share a couple more illustrations to emphasize the importance of following God's directions in order to maintain our freedom in Christ.

On January 13, 1982, a very wintry day in our nation's capital, the crew in a Boeing 737 attempted to leave Washington National Airport. When the plane left the ground, it stalled, crashed into the 14th Street Bridge, and plummeted into the Potomac River.

It was a terrible tragedy accentuated by the weather conditions. The official reports revealed that this accident could have been avoided had the crew used the resources available.

In actuality, the flight crew did not use engine anti-icer during ground operations *or* takeoff. The engine inlet pressure probe on both engines became blocked with ice before initiation of takeoff. Consequently, this led to an erroneous reading of thrust produced.

Sufficient power and thrust were available. But because the instruments were not responding correctly, the crew responded incorrectly and so did the engines. The results were tragic.

And so it is with Christians. We sometimes don't rise above

the "law of sin" because we don't use the resources available to us. We don't follow God's principles and guidelines which He has so clearly outlined in Scripture. Consequently, there are times Christians also crash and burn.

It must be emphasized at this point for those who may have a fear of flying, that the average percent of successful takeoffs and landings in commercial aviation calculates out to 99.999999 percent or more. In actuality, the average American is safer in a modern jet than in his own living room. The statistical probability of experiencing an accident is greater at home than in the air.

The reason is that we can trust God's natural laws. Most aviation accidents happen because of human error. If this is true in the realm of God's natural laws, what about the realm of His spiritual laws? We know what those guidelines and principles are. They are clearly delineated in the Bible. If we follow them and obey them, there is no reason for a Christian to ever "crash and burn" in his Christian life.

To make this point even clearer, let me share another illustration. On December 29, 1972 a large jumbo jet, an L-1011, was approaching the Miami Airport about midnight. An electronic signal indicated possible nose gear problems. The flight engineer descended into the lower section of the plane under the cockpit to check the problem visually. Everything appeared to be normal.

But in the cockpit above, the other crew members were so distracted by this relatively minor problem that they did not realize that the altitude hold feature on the autopilot was not activated. Furthermore, no one was watching the instrument panel. And when they received a radio message from the Miami Control Tower that they had reached an altitude of

900 feet, with a question as to whether everything was in order, the crew responded with an affirmative.

But unknown to the crew, the huge aircraft was slowly descending. And before they knew what happened, slowly but surely the plane continued its descent and crashed into the Florida Everglades.

Again, I think the spiritual lesson is clear. As Christians, we can make a good start in our Christian lives. We obey God's principles and guidelines. We're victorious in our Christian experience. We are on guard against Satan.

But at some point we become careless. We become distracted. We stop consulting the Word of God—particularly when we feel we're in control. We ignore the warnings of our Christian friends. But, unfortunately we are "descending lower and lower" and we can't even perceive it. And before we know what has happened, we end up in a dismal swamp.

There's another more subtle lesson from this illustration. Though our change in thinking and behavior regarding certain spiritual values may be very slight, in a matter of time it can make a great difference. The changes may even be imperceptible. "It won't make that much difference," we rationalize. But one questionable decision often leads to another and then to another. Little by little, we allow ourselves to be brought into bondage to the things of this world. Little by little, we lose our freedom to serve God and others. And before we know it, we're in a spiritual swamp.

Steps to Freedom

In our next chapter we want to develop more fully the relationship between freedom and serving. But it is important to note at this juncture that we cannot serve God and others unless we are truly free in Christ. And to be truly free in Christ, we must take the following steps.

STEP 1. To be truly free in Christ to serve God and others, *I must accept Jesus Christ as my personal Saviour*. He died for me and rose again. I must make this truth personal in my own life.

Have you truly become a Christian? If not, take this step today. This prayer will help you:

> Father, I thank You for sending Jesus Christ into this world to set me free from sin. Thank You that He bore my sins on the cross. Thank You that He rose again, being victorious over death. Thank You that I can be identified with His death and resurrection by believing in what Christ has done. Thank You that I can apply this to my life personally. Right here and now I accept Jesus Christ as my personal Saviour from sin. I believe He died and rose again for me.

STEP 2. To be truly free in Christ to serve God and others, I *must appropriate the reality that I am no longer a slave to sin.* Rather, I am the servant of righteousness. The prison door is open. I can walk out into a brand-new experience of grace and love. The potential is there. The power is there. I only need to appropriate it as a reality.

The following prayer will help you accept and appropriate this truth:

> Lord, I accept the fact that I'm a new creature in Christ. I appropriate this reality. I believe that I have died with Christ and have been raised to a new life.

STEP 3. To be truly free in Christ to serve God and others, *I must obey God.* I must live by God's rules. I must apply His truth daily to my life.

This prayer will help you take this step:

> Father, I offer my body to You as a living, holy, and pleasing sacrifice. This is my spiritual worship. By Your grace I will no longer conform my life to the pattern of this world. Rather, I will renew my mind day by day and be transformed into Christ's image. I commit myself to obey Your will—which I acknowledge is good and pleasing and perfect.

3
Serving in the Spirit

On various occasions over the years I have been involved in confronting Christians face-to-face who have clearly and obviously departed from the will of God. The Bible teaches that it is our spiritual responsibility to attempt to restore Christians who are "caught in a sin" (Gal. 6:1). But it is always a very difficult and awesome task. Thus Paul warned, "*But watch yourself,* or you also may be tempted" (v. 1). In other words, we must always approach this kind of task with a deep sense of humility and caution.

Once I approached a Christian brother who had left his wife and family for another woman. I was not prepared for what I heard and experienced. This man had carefully worked out a scheme in his own mind to justify his actions. Though he still claimed to believe the Bible and what it taught about Jesus Christ and salvation, he had reinterpreted Scripture to make room for his new lifestyle. He had obviously decided to use his "freedom" in Christ to "indulge the sinful nature" (5:13). No amount of effort on my part could convince him his choices would ultimately result in heartache and a broken spirit. Though he knew his wife was desperately hurt and wounded and that his children were disillusioned and bitter and perhaps headed for spiritual disaster, he chose to "gratify the desires of the sinful nature" rather than to "live by the Spirit" (5:16). In fact, he made it clear that he was ready to pay whatever consequences there might be for his choices.

My heart was saddened over this experience. But I was also reminded once again of how easy it is to get sidetracked from doing the will of God and to become a victim of our own selfish desires. Unfortunately, this illustrates what is happening to more and more Christians today who are influenced by the wisdom of the world.

However, this is not a new phenomenon. This is why Paul wrote and cautioned the Galatians, "You, my brothers, were called to be free. *But do not use your freedom to indulge the sinful nature;* rather, serve one another in love" (Gal. 5:13).

How can Christians avoid this trap? How can we use our freedom in Christ responsibly? Paul gives us the answer to these questions in the Galatian letter. "So I say, live by the Spirit, and you *will not* gratify the desires of the sinful nature" (v. 16).

Conflict

Before looking more closely at what Paul means by the injunction to "live by the Spirit," we must remember that when we become true believers in Christ, our sinful nature *is not eliminated.* The old capacity or old nature is still present. And because it is present, there will always be a *conflict* between what our old nature wants and what Christ wants for us. "For the sinful nature desires what is contrary to the Spirit, and the Spirit what is contrary to the sinful nature. They are in *conflict* with each other" (v. 17).

All of us have experienced this tension. To deny it is to deny reality. The Bible teaches it and experience verifies it.

Once the great French preacher, Louis Bourdaloue, was probing the conscience of Louis XIV when he used the words of Paul: "For the good that I would, I do not; but the evil which I would not, that I do" (Rom. 7:19, KJV). He began the application by saying: "I find two men in me. . . ." But the king interrupted the great preacher with the memorable exclamation: "Ah, these two men I know them well!"

The good news, however, is that we need not be controlled by the old nature. We are no longer in bondage to this old capacity. We have been set free. Consequently, it is possible to keep our sin nature subdued and under control. Though we will definitely struggle at times, it need not be one persistent experience filled with tension. We can experience true freedom in Christ when we "live by the Spirit" (Gal. 5:16). This is what Paul meant when he wrote, "The law of the *Spirit of life* set me *free* from the law of sin and death" (Rom. 8:2).

Confusion

At this point, many Christians get confused. What does it mean to "live by the Spirit," or as the *King James Version* is translated, to "walk in the Spirit"?

I can understand this confusion, because as a young Christian and as a young man (I became a Christian at age 16) I became *very* confused. I wanted desperately to please God in my Christian walk. But I immediately began to hear various views on the Holy Spirit. The spiritual leaders in my own religious background had taught me I would receive the Holy Spirit after I was baptized in water and when the elders of the church placed their hands on me and prayed for me. However, I knew something was wrong with this doctrine because I found illustrations in Scripture where the Holy Spirit came upon people apart from any human instrumentality (Acts 2:1-4; 10:44-46). In good conscience I had to reject that view because I believed I received the Spirit of God when I became a Christian—when I trusted Christ as my Saviour. Paul's words to the Corinthians summed it up for me, "For we were *all* baptized by one Spirit into one body—whether Jews or Greeks, slave or free—and we were all given the one Spirit to drink" (1 Cor. 12:13).

Shortly after I became a Christian, a fellow student in high school, knowing I had become a believer, began to tell me that I needed to be "baptized in the Spirit" in order to be a dynamic Christian. And if I were baptized and filled in this way, I would then "speak in tongues"—a sign of my baptism and filling.

Being a new Christian and very untaught, this launched me into a study of Scripture regarding this idea. I also attended several meetings where people claimed to have this experience. I was open to any experience God might have for me. I really wanted to be a strong Christian.

After a period of personal Bible study and interaction with other Christians, I concluded something was seriously wrong with this doctrine as well. I certainly discovered some Christians in the New Testament spoke in tongues when they were "filled with the Spirit," but it became clear to me that the Bible did not teach that it was an experience for *all* Christians. Nor was it always a sign of spiritual maturity. In fact, I discovered that the Corinthian Christians spoke in tongues more than anybody else (1:4-6), but they were described as one of the most carnal and worldly churches in the New Testament (3:1-3).

I must quickly add that this is not an indictment of all charismatics. Some of the most mature Christians I have ever met over the years claim to have had this experience. Conversely, some of the most immature Christians I've met are non-charismatics who are very judgmental of charismatics. There is maturity and immaturity in every Bible-believing church—charismatic and non-charismatic. However, my own study of Scripture has led me to conclude that some aspects of both charismatic theology and non-charismatic regarding the Holy Spirit are not biblically accurate.

Over the years I've seen many Christians confused regarding the doctrine of the Holy Spirit. Many go through the same process I went through.

WHAT DOES THE BIBLE TEACH ABOUT THE HOLY SPIRIT? First, a proper relationship with the Holy Spirit is very important in enabling us to avoid indulging the sinful nature and to be able to serve others in love. In fact, to "serve one another in love" and to "serve in the Spirit" are inseparable concepts. This is clear from the passage we're studying in the Galatian letter (Gal. 5:13-18).

Why the confusion? A major reason is that we do not distinguish between what is a *normative* experience with the Holy Spirit and what is a *unique* experience with the Holy Spirit. In Galatians, Paul is referring to a normative experience—an experience for *all believers* of *all time*. In fact, this is what is taught in *all* the letters written to the churches. The Book of Acts, on the other hand, records several events that describe a *unique experience* with the Holy Spirit. We get confused when we "confuse" the two experiences. Let me illustrate what I mean.

NORMATIVE EXPERIENCE. In this passage from Galatians, Paul describes this experience in three different ways:

- Live by the Spirit (5:16)
- Be led by the Spirit (5:18)
- Keep in step with the Spirit (5:25)

In the Roman letter, Paul describes this experience in two additional ways:

- Live according to the Spirit (Rom. 8:4)
- Have the mind controlled by the Spirit (8:6)

In the Ephesian letter, Paul states it yet differently:

- Be filled with the Spirit (Eph. 5:18)

It is this command in the Ephesian letter that often opens the door to confusion, especially if we take Paul's exhortation out of context. The reason is that the terminology used in this verse from Ephesians is the same basic terminology used in Acts to describe *unique experiences* with the Holy Spirit.

UNIQUE EXPERIENCES. Following are the basic historical statements from the Book of Acts that describe these unique experiences with the Holy Spirit:

- On the Day of Pentecost, the 12 Apostles "were *filled* with the Holy Spirit and began to speak in other tongues as the Spirit enabled them" (Acts 1:26; 2:4).

- When Peter and John were questioned by the

rulers, elders, and teachers of the law, Peter responded. He was "*filled* with the Holy Spirit" as he responded to their questioning (4:8).

- When Peter and John were released from their interrogation, they reported what had happened. All of those gathered to hear their report were "*filled* with the Holy Spirit and spoke the Word of God boldly" (4:31).

- The seven men chosen to serve the widows in Acts 6 were known to be "*full* of the Spirit" (6:3, 5, 8; 7:55).

- The Apostle Paul was "*filled* with the Holy Spirit" following his conversion to Christ on the road to Damascus (9:17).

- Barnabas was recognized as a man "*full* of the Holy Spirit" (11:24).

- Paul was "*filled* with the Holy Spirit" when he confronted Elymas, the sorcerer, and pronounced blindness upon him (13:9).

Contrasts

As we look at the *prescriptive* statements in Paul's epistles regarding a Christian's experience with the Holy Spirit as well as at the *descriptive* events in the Book of Acts, we can notice some significant differences and contrasts. Some of these contrasts are as follows:

Unique Experiences Described in the Book of Acts	*Normative Experiences Described in the Epistles*
• *Often* associated with *special tasks* and the power to work miracles. (Note context of each statement in the Book of Acts.)	• *Always* associated with *living the Christian life* from day to day. (Note context of each statement in the Epistles.)
• Focuses on *God's sovereign grace* in bringing about this experience. (Note that in Acts it was an external happening bestowed by God on certain occasions.)	• Focuses on *man's responsibility* to obey God's revealed will. (Note that in the Epistles it is clear that individual Christians can control this experience.)
• *Often* related to *certain Christians*. (Such as the apostles, Peter, Stephen, Philip, Barnabas, Paul, etc.)	• *Always* related to *all believers*.
• Was an experience that was *repeated* in the lives of certain Christians for special tasks. (For example, the apostles were filled on the Day of Pentecost and were later filled	• Was to be a *consistent* day-by-day experience for all Christians. (Again, note the context of the statements in the Epistles.)

for other special tasks; Paul was filled in a special way to confront Elymas.)

- Usually described with the words "to be *filled*"; "*full* of," etc.

- Described with a *variety of words* and phrases. (Note that the words "be filled" are used only once in the Epistles, Eph. 5:18.)

Conclusions

What then does Paul mean in the Galatian letter to "live by the Spirit"? It means to be obedient to the truth the Spirit has revealed. This is why Jesus, speaking of the coming of the Holy Spirit, referred to the third Person of the Trinity three times as "the Spirit of Truth" (John 14:17; 15:26; 16:13).

More specifically, it means to allow God's Word to permeate our lives so that the Holy Spirit, who lives in every true believer, can lead us and guide us. This is why Paul wrote, "Let the *Word of Christ* dwell in you richly as you teach and admonish one another with all wisdom, and as you sing psalms, hymns, and spiritual songs with gratitude in your hearts to God" (Col. 3:16).

This is a parallel passage with Paul's statement in the Ephesian letter where he admonished all believers to "be filled with the Spirit" (Eph. 5:18-19).

Who and what is the "Word of Christ"? It refers to that which is both *living* and *written*. Jesus Christ is the Living Word (John 1:1, 14). So is the Holy Spirit. And often the Bible interchangeably refers to Jesus Christ *and* the Holy Spirit, who lives within us (e.g., Rom. 8:9-10).

However, the Spirit of Christ, who lives within us, is closely associated with the "written Word of Christ" as we have it today in the Bible. In fact, the Holy Spirit is the author of Scripture. He inspired men to record for us God's divine truth: "All Scripture is God-breathed and is useful" (2 Tim. 3:16-17; 2 Peter 1:20-21). Therefore, the Holy Spirit is the One who aids us in understanding Scripture and more importantly, appropriating that truth from Scripture into our own lives. In fact, it is dangerous to follow any internal leading if we don't test that leading against Scripture's teaching. One thing for sure, the Holy Spirit never contradicts the written Word of God.

To "be filled with the Spirit" then means to allow the "Word of Christ to dwell in us richly." When this happens, there is a definite interaction in our hearts between the *Person* of the Holy Spirit and the *truth* He has revealed in written form.

There are no simple formulas for living the Christian life. To "be filled with the Spirit" means:

- that we don't let sin reign in our mortal bodies (Rom. 6:12).
- offering the parts of our bodies to God as "instruments of righteousness" (6:13).
- being daily transformed by the renewing of our minds (12:2).
- living a life worthy of the calling to which we have been called (Eph. 4:1).
- putting off our "old self" and putting on the "new self" (4:22-24).
- being an imitator of God and living a life of love as He loved us (Eph. 5:1-2).

Inseparable Concepts

It is clear from Galatians 5:16 that we cannot "serve one another in love" unless we have a proper relationship with the Holy Spirit. In fact, "serving in the Spirit" and "serving one another in love" are inseparable concepts.

PERSONAL QUESTION. *Do I have a proper relationship with the Holy Spirit?* If I do not, I will not "serve others" as I should. Rather, I will indulge my sinful nature in my relationships with others. I will use people for my own ends.

COUNTER QUESTION. *What does it mean to have a proper relationship with the Holy Spirit?* Paul answers this question succinctly in his Roman letter.

> Those who live according to the sinful nature have their minds set on what that nature desires; but those *who live in accordance with the Spirit have their minds set on what the Spirit desires* (Rom. 8:5).

To live in proper relationship with the Holy Spirit means to focus our minds on the Holy Spirit's thoughts and desires. And there's only one trustworthy source in which we can find what the Spirit of God thinks and wants for all Christians. That source is the revealed will of God in the Holy Scriptures.

A FINAL THOUGHT. Remember that the Father, Son, and Holy Spirit operate in concert with one another. They are three Persons, yet one God. Our relationship with the Holy Spirit indicates our relationship with the heavenly Father. Jesus said, "God is Spirit, and His worshipers must worship in spirit and in truth" (John 4:24).

Furthermore, our relationship with the Holy Spirit indicates our relationship with our Saviour, Jesus Christ. In writing to the Roman Christians, Paul said:

You, however, are controlled not by the sinful nature but by the Spirit, if the Spirit of God lives in you. And if anyone does not have the Spirit of Christ, he does not belong to Christ. But *if Christ is in you*, your body is dead because of sin, yet your spirit is alive because of righteousness. And *if the Spirit* of Him who raised Jesus from the dead *is living in you,* He who raised Christ from the dead will also give life to your mortal bodies through His Spirit, who lives in you (Rom. 8:9-11).

4
Servants of Righteousness

My attention was caught this past week by Bob St. John's editorial in the *Dallas Morning News* entitled, "Of Manners, Respect and Consideration for Others" (March 14, 1983, p. 15-A). Bob was sitting in a restaurant with a friend. They noticed what he described as a "big, chubby guy" sitting at a table with a young lady. "The big, chubby guy just sat there smiling glassy eyed," Bob observed. "One time he seemed to be cranking up to say something but, apparently, the moment passed or the light bulb went out in his head."

Continuing, Bob reported that the "guy just kept reaching over and hugging" the young lady. "She'd just lean against him, looking blank."

" 'Hey,' he finally said. 'You ready? Let's go,' then he smiled as if he knew a secret. He got up and started walking out."

The young lady got up and followed the guy through the door. But about 30 minutes later, the young lady reappeared—*without* her chubby friend. Asked what happened, she reported, " 'We went in separate cars. He was following me to my apartment, but I made a quick turn and managed to lose him. He's a creep anyway.' "

A few minutes later, however, the "big, chubby guy" also reappeared on the scene. " 'Oh, hi,' said the young lady. 'What happened to you? I was worried.' "

Why this illustration? When I read it I couldn't help but think of Paul's exhortation to the Galatians to "serve one another." It illustrates that all of life is relational. What this woman was saying, of course, was untrue. On the one hand, she didn't like the guy. She probably knew he was going to use her for selfish reasons. She had been down that road before. On the other hand, from an emotional perspective, she probably needed another human being in her life. She wanted a relationship, superficial though it might be. On this particular evening she somehow convinced herself she could do better.

Life Is Relational

As people, we are part of a human family. Whether a woman lives in a playboy mansion, or in a convent; whether she is a wife, or a mistress—she is obligated to and dependent on someone else—at least one other person and usually more. Whether a man is a corporate executive, or a pastor; whether he is President of the United States, or the leader of a local drug ring—he *must relate* to others. It is impossible to live apart from some kind of human relationship that has certain reciprocal responsibilities. We do not—and we cannot—live in isolation from one another. We are dependent on each other to meet one another's needs—physically, emotionally, socially—and yes, spiritually.

This is by design—God's design. It has been true from the beginning of time. It's even true in the world of animals. Let me illustrate.

The animal inhabitant of the Pinna Marina is a blind slug or snail, who has many enemies. His worst enemy is the cuttlefish. If the Pinna opens his shell, the cuttlefish will rush in and devour him. How then can such a blind, defenseless creature secure food and protect himself?

Fortunately there is a crab fish who is a constant companion of the Pinna. They live together in a Pinna's shell. When the Pinna is hungry, he opens his valves and sends out his faithful companion to secure food. If an enemy approaches, the watchful crab dashes back to his blind protector, who quickly closes the valves as soon as his friend is inside.

On the other hand, when the crab returns with food and there are no enemies crouching nearby, he will make a gentle noise at the opening of the Pinna's shell, which has been closed during the crab's absence. When the Pinna hears this noise, he opens his shell, the crab enters and the two friends then feast together on the fruits of the crab's industry.

Even more intriguing is the ratel, a badger-like animal. Together, he meets his needs in cooperation with a small bird who loves honey. When they're hungry, they go out together. The keen eye of the little bird quickly pinpoints a beehive with honey. Then the ratel with his powerful claws tears up the hive, making the honey available to both of them.

It should not surprise us that in human life, dependent relationships are even more important. When God created Adam, He said, "It is not good for the man to be alone. I will make a helper suitable for him" (Gen. 2:18). Consequently,

God created a woman for Adam. This began the human family and its reciprocal responsibilities.

As believers in Jesus Christ, we are part of a *unique* family—the family of God. Not only is it a family with human dimensions, but with divine dimensions as well. And when Paul exhorted the Galatian Christians to "serve one another in love" (5:13), he was well aware of the relational realities of life, both in the human family as well as in the Christian family. Thus, before he issued this "serving" directive, he wrote, "Do not use your freedom to indulge the sinful nature" (v. 13).

You see, Adam and Eve sinned by disobeying God. They brought a curse on the whole human race. Ever since then, every human being has had to deal with a sinful nature. In fact, Paul said we became "*slaves to sin,* which leads to death" (Rom. 6:16). But in Christ we "have been set free from sin and have become slaves to righteousness" (v. 18). Put in very practical terms, we will either serve one another as we "indulge the sinful nature," or we will serve one another as we are led by God's Holy Spirit. If we serve others by indulging the sinful nature, we will do so primarily out of self-centered and carnal reasons. If we serve others according to God's Spirit, we will do so with motives that are God centered and oriented toward the other person's good. If we serve one another with selfish motives, our behavior becomes unrighteous. But if we serve one another in love, following the leadership of the *Holy* Spirit, we will relate to one another in *righteous* and *holy* ways. And as members of God's family we are to be "servants of righteousness," not unrighteousness.

It's clear then that we all have needs—deep needs. Some of

them are physical, some emotional, some social, and some spiritual. This introduces us to some very practical questions.

1. How can I as a Christian learn to "live by the Spirit" in my relationships with others?
2. How can I continue to serve others when they don't reciprocate?
3. How can I relate to others in unselfish ways and still keep my motives right and pure regarding my own needs?

Paul addresses these questions in Galatians 5. After exhorting Christians to "serve one another in love," he describes how to recognize behavior that reflects the sinful nature.

The Acts of the Sinful Nature

When Paul wrote to the Galatians, he stated that "the acts of the sinful nature are obvious" (5:19). Sin permeated their lifestyle before they became believers. They knew what the acts of the sinful nature were. But just to make the record clear for the Galatians—and for Christians of all time—Paul lists them (vv. 19-21). They are as follows:

Sexual Immorality	Fits of Rage
Impurity	Selfish Ambition
Debauchery	Dissensions
Idolatry	Factions
Witchcraft	Envy
Hatred	Drunkenness
Discord	Orgies
Jealousy	

"I warn you," Paul continued, "as I did before, that those who live like this will not inherit the kingdom of God" (v. 21).

Does Paul mean by this final statement that a person who "indulges the sinful nature" in any of these areas cannot be a Christian? Furthermore, does he mean that a Christian who indulges his sinful nature in some of these areas will lose his salvation?

The answer is no. Rather, Paul is saying that this is the *lifestyle* of those who do not know Christ. But in this passage in Galatians, he is also saying that a true Christian *will be tempted* to "gratify the desires of the sinful nature" (v. 16). That will always be a reality until we are with Christ in heaven. However, he is also saying by implication that a true believer who loves Christ and others will not continue to be a "slave to sin" and to the "old nature." A true believer will become in actuality a "slave to righteousness." He will use his freedom to serve others in love rather than to serve others selfishly and in fleshly and carnal ways.

Paul summarized this concept clearly in his Roman letter:

> Therefore, brothers, we have an obligation—but it is not to the sinful nature, to live according to it. For if you live according to the sinful nature, you will die; but if by the Spirit you put to death the misdeeds of the body, you will live, because those who are led by the Spirit of God *are sons of God* (Rom. 8:12-14).

The Fruit of the Spirit

How do we recognize Christians who "live by the Spirit"? They will manifest the fruit of the Spirit in their relationships with others. Paul outlines these qualities next (Gal. 5:22-23). In his prayer for the Philippians, he identifies these qualities as the "fruit of righteousness" (Phil. 1:11):

Love
Joy
Peace
Patience
Kindness
Goodness
Faithfulness
Gentleness
Self-control

These qualities are in stark contrast to the "acts of the old nature." And so Paul concludes, "Since we *live by the Spirit*, let us *keep in step with the Spirit*. Let us not become conceited, provoking and envying each other" (Gal. 5:25-26).

For years, Christians have "emotionalized" this passage. We have erroneously believed that if we are "filled with the Spirit," certain feelings will be generated in our inner beings—*feelings* of love, *feelings* of joy, *feelings* of peace, *feelings* of patience, etc. Not so! Certainly it is the will of God that a Christian who lives by the Spirit by keeping in step with the Spirit will *enjoy* the experience. Often, however, feelings are the reward that come with obedience. Feelings are not in themselves the basic motivation. For example, I have not been motivated with a *feeling* of patience or a *feeling* of self-control. Rather, I have been motivated to manifest these qualities toward others because they are what the Holy Spirit wants in my life. And when I obey, I feel good about pleasing God and keeping in step with the Spirit.

A "Bird's-Eye View"

It is important at this point that we get the big picture regarding Paul's emphasis in this passage. Paul's main concern is that we serve one another in love rather than serving one another in carnal and fleshly ways. Therefore, we must see the acts of the sinful nature as primarily *relational* in nature. In fact, the whole passage (Gal. 5:13-26) is *relational* in nature.

Why is this true? Because all of life is relational. If we follow the old nature, our relationships with others can very quickly become *immoral, impure, and idolatrous.* Relationships can reflect *hatred, discord, jealousy and fits of rage, selfish ambition, dissensions, and factions.* No one would deny that all of these concepts are relational in nature, but oriented toward self.

By contrast, if we serve one another in love, we will meet one another's needs in unselfish ways. The results will be *more love* among us. People will be *joyful and happy.* There will be a sense of *peace, tranquillity, and unity.* We will treat one another with *patience and kindness.* We will do what is *right* in our relationships. We will be *faithful* to one another according to the guidelines of Scripture. We will treat each other with *gentleness* and exercise *self-control* so that we don't use people for our own selfish ends.

If we live by the Spirit we'll reflect the fruit of the Spirit and our relationships will be characterized by *righteousness.* Thus, to be a servant to others in love, we must first of all be servants of righteousness. For it is our commitment to following the leadership of God's Holy Spirit that keeps serving others from becoming a relational trap.

Some Personal Questions

> How can Christians learn to live by the Spirit in their relationships with one another rather than indulging their sinful nature?

The basic answer is that in the home and the church we all need both *models* and direct *teaching.*

Modeling is foundational to helping others live by the

Spirit. Paul wrote to the Corinthians—a very carnal church—and said, "Follow my example, as I follow the example of Christ" (1 Cor. 11:1). Paul never asked people to do something that he himself was not doing.

Modeling is necessary both in the family and in the church. To the fathers Paul wrote, "Fathers, do not exasperate your children." That's the model. However, Paul said, "Instead, bring them up in the *training* and *instruction* of the Lord" (Eph. 6:4). That's teaching.

Paul loved to combine the home with the church. And when he wrote to the Thessalonians, we see once again this blend—but we also see the modeling and the teaching process. "You are witnesses, and so is God, of how holy, righteous, and blameless we were among you who believed." Here we see the model. But Paul, drawing from the illustration of the home, went on to say, "For you know that we dealt with each of you as a *father* deals with his own children, *encouraging, comforting,* and *urging* you to live lives worthy of God, who calls you into His kingdom and glory" (1 Thes. 2:10-11).

Paul also made the same point when he wrote to young Timothy who was doing pastoral work at Ephesus. *"Set an example* for the believers in speech, in life, in love, in faith, and in purity" (1 Tim. 4:12). But immediately Paul followed the modeling process with the exhortation to teach. "Until I come," Paul wrote, "devote yourself to the public reading of Scripture, to *preaching* and to *teaching*" (v. 13).

A few sentences later, Paul put it all together. "Be diligent in these matters; give yourself wholly to them, so that everyone may *see* your progress. Watch your *life* and *doctrine* closely" (vv. 15-16).

The greatest model, however, is not just an individual Christian—a Paul, a Timothy, or an individual elder in your church or mine. Rather it's the *whole body* of believers. Paul made this clear in his letter to the Thessalonians. "You became imitators of us and of the Lord; in spite of severe suffering, you welcomed the message with the joy given by the Holy Spirit. And so you became a *model* to all the believers in Macedonia and Achaia" (1 Thes. 1:6-7).

God then wants every local body of believers to become a model of what it means to live by the Spirit, reflecting the fruit of the Spirit in all of our relationships.

> How can we serve others when they tend to serve themselves and don't reciprocate? They receive, but seldom respond!

The answer is to keep on loving, keep on modeling, keep on speaking the truth in love. We must not allow discouragement to cause us to cease serving others in love.

There is a point, of course, beyond which Christians should not go, especially in individual relationships. To give when others do not respond, in actuality is often a test of our motives. If we do not serve others because they do not serve us, our motives may have been selfish in the first place. It indicates that our eyes are on ourselves and others rather than on the God we serve. We must remember that if we serve to be rewarded down here, we may lose our reward in heaven.

Don't misunderstand. God wants us to be rewarded down here. He wants us to enjoy the response that comes from service. But if our primary motive is to serve in order to be served, we have already reversed the process. Jesus said He came to minister, not to be ministered unto (Matt. 20:28).

We are to follow Christ's example.

> How can we relate to others in unselfish ways and still keep our motives regarding our needs right and pure?

There's only one way to keep this process in proper focus—we must "serve one another in *love.*" True Christlike love is the guiding principle. Love puts the other person first—no matter what our needs. When all Christians put other Christians first, our own needs *will* be met far beyond anything we could ever imagine.

WARNING: God does not want us to go around questioning our motives in an obsessive fashion. Personal needs are a reality. And God designed the family of God so that we might meet each other's needs. If we "serve in love," we'll not use each other for our own ends. If we "live by the Spirit," our relationships will be reciprocal for the glory of God. This is why Paul wrote, "Submit to one another out of reverence for Christ" (Eph. 5:21).

What about You?

How are you relating to others? Your needs are important, but are you using others selfishly? Are you indulging your old nature? Are you allowing others to serve you without your serving them? Or, are you following God's Holy Spirit? You can check yourself. Paul's two lists will help you be very specific. Check those areas that characterize your relationships with others. If you are honest, you will soon determine if you are a servant of righteousness or a servant of unrighteousness in your dealings with others.

In using the lists, remember that the "acts of the sinful nature" reflect a lifestyle given over to carnal living. Christians will not continue to live this way when they are exposed to God's truth. However, it is possible for true Christians to "indulge the sinful nature," just as the Corinthians did. But when they were confronted with their sins, the Corinthians eventually responded to God's truth. It is the will of God that we follow the desires of the Holy Spirit rather than the desires of our old nature.

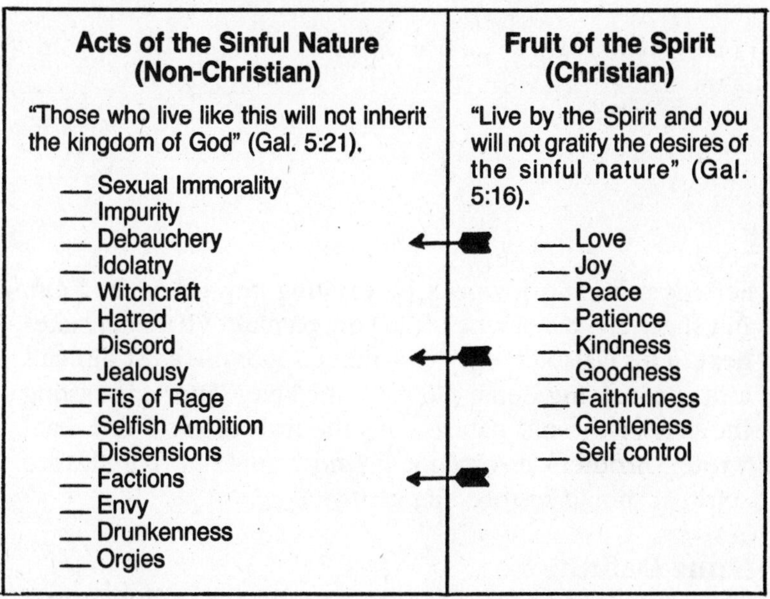

Acts of the Sinful Nature (Non-Christian)	Fruit of the Spirit (Christian)
"Those who live like this will not inherit the kingdom of God" (Gal. 5:21).	"Live by the Spirit and you will not gratify the desires of the sinful nature" (Gal. 5:16).
___ Sexual Immorality ___ Impurity ___ Debauchery ___ Idolatry ___ Witchcraft ___ Hatred ___ Discord ___ Jealousy ___ Fits of Rage ___ Selfish Ambition ___ Dissensions ___ Factions ___ Envy ___ Drunkenness ___ Orgies	___ Love ___ Joy ___ Peace ___ Patience ___ Kindness ___ Goodness ___ Faithfulness ___ Gentleness ___ Self control

A Prayer Goal

Dear Father, help me to stop indulging my sinful nature and help me to serve others in love. Help me to live by the Spirit, manifesting the fruit of the Spirit in my relationships with others. Since I live by the Spirit, help me to keep in step with the Spirit. In Jesus' name, Amen.

5

The True Test of Servanthood

Serving others in love can be exciting, rewarding, and fun. But there are times when it is very painful. What Paul states next in his Galatian letter is without doubt the most difficult aspect of serving. Some call it "tough love." After contrasting the acts of the old nature with the fruit of the Spirit, Paul wrote, "Brothers, if someone is *caught* in a sin, you who are spiritual should restore him gently" (Gal. 6:1).

Some Definitions

Three words should be defined before we look at Paul's main concern in this passage. The first word is *caught;* the second is *sin;* and the third is *spiritual.*

CAUGHT. To be "caught in a sin" can be interpreted two ways. We can get *caught* with our hand in the cookie jar, or we can be so *caught up* in a sin that try as we might, we can't keep our hand out of the cookie jar.

When I was about 13 or 14 years old, I talked my parents into letting me stay home from church one Sunday, supposedly to listen to a Christian radio program for children. Actually, I wanted to go see a girl who was visiting a friend of mine who lived on a farm several miles up the road. So as soon as my parents headed off for church, I jumped in my dad's old '34 Ford truck to carry out my plan.

My friend lived on a farm off the highway, and to get there you had to take a dirt road. For several weeks it had been raining and the ditches on both sides of the road were filled with water.

But this all figured into my little scheme, you see, because I knew my friend and his cute little blonde cousin were in a swimming hole way back in the field. So I put that old truck in "fast forward." Unfortunately, while laying one hand on the old "uga" horn to announce my arrival and steering with the other, I lost complete control of the truck. It skidded sideways and ended up head-on in one of the side ditches. The engine immediately stalled and when I tried to start it, it was so submerged that water shot out of the exhaust pipe.

I was never so scared in my life. My exhilaration turned to humiliation. Knowing my father would be home in a couple of hours, I ran all the way home, got the tractor, and with the help of my friend's older brother, pulled the truck out of the ditch. However, there was no way it would start, so he pulled me all the way home. To make matters worse, I burned up the clutch trying to start the engine. About five minutes before we pulled into my own driveway, my folks had arrived home—and my dad was waiting on the front lawn.

No doubt about it! I was *caught* with my hand in the cookie jar. I'll leave the rest to your imagination. I will say this, however, I'm glad Paul said, "Brother, if someone is caught in a sin, you who are spiritual should restore him *gently.*" Fortunately for me, my dad was a *gentle* man.

What Paul shares in this passage applies equally to both parenting and pastoring. Because we're not perfect as Christians, we find ourselves breaking rules—more specifically violating God's spiritual laws. In a moment of weakness we yield to temptation—and get caught. But far more seriously, there is the person who is caught in sin and can't seem to break away. Fortunately for me, lying to my parents never became a habit. If it had, I would have been *trapped* in a sin, not just caught on a single occasion.

SIN. When Paul used the word *sin* in Galatians 6:1, he was referring to an earlier paragraph in which he had already enumerated what these various sins might be. They are identified as the "acts of the sinful nature" (5:19-21). It might be a sexual sin. It might be some form of idolatry—for example, materialism. It might be some kind of witchcraft, in our culture frequently related to drugs. It might be anger or jealousy, often twin emotions. It might be self-centered behavior. It might be a divisive nature, always creating disunity. It might be envy or drunkenness.

SPIRITUAL. Paul had also defined what he meant by being *spiritual.* Those who are spiritual should restore the person who is caught in sin. This is a task for those who "live by the Spirit" (5:16); those who are "led by the Spirit" (v. 18); and those who "keep in step with the Spirit" (v. 25). Paul had delineated clearly how to recognize people who are spiritual—they manifest the fruit of the Spirit in their relationships—"love, joy, peace, patience, kindness, goodness, faithfulness, gentleness, and self-control" (vv. 22-23).

Restoration—Not Condemnation

What should a Christian's attitudes and actions be toward another believer who has indulged his sinful nature and is caught or trapped? "Restore him," Paul said. This should be our primary concern and goal.

Unfortunately, Christians are often too quick to judge, too quick to condemn, and too quick to isolate and alienate the "sinner." Don't misunderstand. Christians are often too quick to overlook sin and do nothing about it. This is also wrong.

But we must always remember that the primary purpose for church discipline—of any discipline—is *restoration,* not condemnation and isolation. If we keep this goal in our own hearts, it will affect our attitudes and actions toward those who fail in their Christian experience.

Jesus Christ Himself is the greatest example in this area. My favorite story is from John 8. The Jewish leaders brought a woman to Jesus who was "*caught* in adultery" (8:3). Totally insensitive to what little dignity this woman may have had left, they accused her publicly before the group that Jesus was teaching. "Teacher," they said, "this woman was caught in the act of adultery. In the Law Moses commanded us to stone such women. Now what do You say?" (vv. 4-5)

John tells us these Jewish leaders were trying to trap Jesus (v. 6). They could have cared less about this woman's spiritual welfare and restoration.

Jesus handled this episode magnificently. While they were accusing her, He remained silent. He simply bent down and began "to write on the ground with His finger" (v. 6).

However, they kept questioning Him. Jesus straightened up and said, " 'If any one of you is without sin, let him be the first to throw a stone at her.' Again He stooped down and wrote on the ground" (vv. 7-8). Something strange happened. One by one the men walked away, "the older ones first, until only Jesus was left, with the woman standing there" (v. 9).

Jesus asked her where her accusers had gone and if they had taken steps to stone her. Of course, no one had.

Jesus' response was beautiful. "Then neither do I condemn you. Go now and leave your life of sin" (v. 11).

Have you ever wondered why these men left—the older ones first? Have you ever wondered what Jesus wrote in the sand? We can only speculate. My theory is that He began to write the names of every woman those men had sinned against—beginning with the older men—maybe even including the specific time factors. Furthermore, they also trapped themselves, because if this woman had been caught in the act of adultery, then where was the man? Why didn't they bring him too? He was also guilty of violating the Law of Moses.

And this leads us to another theory. The very man may have been standing there. If so, Jesus would have also written his name in the sand.

Whatever, Jesus demonstrated beautifully what Paul wrote in Galatians, "Brothers, if someone is caught in a sin, you who are spiritual should restore him gently" (Gal. 6:1).

This leads us to what Paul outlines as guidelines for carrying out this process of restoration.

Guidelines for Restoration

Paul outlines at least four guidelines for attempting to restore a person who is caught in sin.

YOU WHO ARE SPIRITUAL. Restoring a person who is caught in sin is a task for Christians who have their own spiritual act together. This is what makes it such a difficult task. Who among us feels up to this responsibility?

Jesus also spoke to this issue with a rather graphic illustration. Before we attempt to take a speck of sawdust out of a brother's eye, we should take the two-by-four out of our own. Don't misunderstand. Jesus was not saying we should not attempt to take the splinter out of a brother's eye. Rather, He was saying we should take the two-by-four out of our own eye so we can see the splinter (Matt. 7:3-5).

This is also why parenting is such an awesome task. How many times as Christian parents do we expect behavior from our children that we do not practice ourselves? What right do we have to correct our children and restore them when we need correction and restoration ourselves? This is why it is so important for parents to "live by the Spirit" and manifest the "fruit of the Spirit."

YOU WHO ARE SPIRITUAL. This guideline is more subtle in Paul's statement. The apostle actually used a plural pronoun here. Consequently, he was referring to more than one "spiritual person" being involved in the restoring process.

There are times when restoration must involve more than one person. Keep in mind that Paul is not talking about those cases where a Christian has sinned against his brother and that brother should approach that Christian alone (Matt. 18:15-17). And if he doesn't respond, then the Christian brother should take one or two other believers with him to try and work out the problem with the first Christian.

Rather, Paul was referring to a person who is caught in sin. His sin is not against you or me, but against God, himself, another person, and the whole body of Christ. In some instances it is even dangerous to approach that person one-on-one, for you cannot predict his response. If he is not open to correction, he may lie, start a rumor, or misinterpret what you say and the way in which you say it. Furthermore, it often takes more than one spiritual person to communicate with an individual who is caught and trapped and defending his sin.

RESTORE HIM GENTLY. Gentleness is a key to communication with any person—no matter how serious the sin. This does not mean that there should not be firmness, directness, and straightforward communication and confrontation. In fact, there must be if the person is initially unresponsive. However, even in confrontation we must always manifest the fruit of the Spirit.

WATCH YOURSELF. Any time we attempt to restore an erring brother or sister, we must be careful that we don't get trapped ourselves. This is what makes this Christian responsibility so awesome.

The most dangerous trap is pride. Any time we attempt to restore someone who is trapped in sin, we will be tempted to think more highly of ourselves than we ought to think (Rom. 12:3). This is why Paul warns, "If anyone thinks he is something when he is nothing, he deceives himself" (Gal. 6:3).

No Christian who knows how subtle Satan is will take this point lightly, including parents. We often get caught in this trap. I've seen some mothers and fathers criticize other parents because of the problems they are facing with their children. In doing so, they set themselves up as examples because their own children are so well behaved. And lo and behold, eventually some have faced the very same problems in their own families. This becomes a very humbling experience indeed! And what's even worse is the young couple without children who, with a sense of pride, let older couples know that their children—when they have them—will not misbehave. I cringe every time I hear a young couple say this directly or indirectly.

Some Personal Questions

Who is responsible to carry out this process?

Every Christian who is spiritual should be involved in the ministry of restoration. And since Paul exhorts every Christian to "live by the Spirit," every believer should eventually be able to help another believer to become a more spiritual Christian. In other words, Paul is not referring to just those who are spiritual leaders in the church. And, of course, being involved in the process of family life makes this a universal responsibility for all parents.

We must remember also that spirituality should not be defined in "either/or" terms. There are degrees of spirituality. Most Christians are strong in some areas and weak in others. All of us can help the weak in areas where we are strong, and even in areas where we are vulnerable ourselves. In the process, however, we must be cautious not to allow Satan to get a foothold in our lives, particularly in the area of pride. This is our enemy's target area because he knows pride comes before a fall.

For example, a person may have trouble with alcohol. In fact, he may be an alcoholic. But, he is no longer in bondage to this spiritual, psychological, and physical weakness. On the other hand, he may not be a strong spiritual Christian in all other areas of his life. This does not disqualify him from helping another person in his own area of weakness. But he must be careful to guard against indulging his sinful nature in this area of weakness.

When should more than one Christian be involved in the restoration process?

In most cases this is necessary when the problems are of a more serious nature—such as moral problems, cases of extreme anger, drug abuse, and alcoholism, etc.

Having more than one person applies particularly in the area of sexual sin. Christians who are particularly weak in this area in their lives should be especially on guard when trying to help a person who has a similar problem. In fact, experience shows that people who are vulnerable in this area should either avoid trying to help another Christian who is weak sexually or should only approach the erring person with several other strong Christians.

Furthermore, people who are involved in sexual sins are extremely prone to rationalization and outright lying. They will often go to great lengths to protect themselves, even attempting to retaliate by attacking another person's character—thus getting the attention off themselves.

I remember very clearly being involved in confronting a Christian leader because of his sexual indiscretions. To my amazement, I discovered that this individual was guilty of this indiscretion at the very same time he had been confronting me about weaknesses in my own life. In retrospect, it appears that he was trying to get the focus off himself. Fortunately, several mature Christians were involved with me in this confrontation and in later confrontations with this man.

Consider another area of caution. Today, many Christians are being taught that a lot of sin problems stem from direct demonic control. And it is true that demons are a reality. It is also true that a lot of problems—no doubt most of them in our culture—stem from sin that has affected us psychologically.

Let me illustrate why it is vital to differentiate between psychological problems and problems caused by direct satanic influence. One evening, following a church service, I encountered a young man who was extremely disturbed. He was in great emotional agony and asked that I pray for him. He told me he felt that he was possessed by a demon.

There were several other pastors who were present at this time and I asked them to join me in prayer for this young man. One of the pastors volunteered to take charge of the situation, indicating that he had had previous experience casting out demons. I more than willingly turned the problem over to him and simply observed the process.

After approximately an hour of what was supposed to be an exorcism, the young man was getting worse. His frustration was increasing and the contortions of his body and speech were very noticeable. During this process, however, I made a number of observations that had distinct psychological overtones. I asked if I might talk to the boy. I knelt down beside him and began to interpret his problems psychologically on the basis of the data I had put together while watching him. His reactions were immediate and, in fact, he appeared shocked at my insight. "Is God telling you what I am thinking?" he asked in a startled manner. "No," I said, "I'm simply interpreting your problem psychologically."

From that moment on, the boy relaxed. When he had gained control of himself, I asked him why he had gone through his previous contortions. His answer was more startling than his quick recovery. He said he did not want to disappoint us. If we thought he had a demon, he wanted to conform to our expectations. He had heard an evangelist talk about casting out demons. Furthermore, the speaker had described very vividly how demons control people. This impressionable young man had identified his inner psychological and spiritual struggles with what the evangelist had described as demon possession and was attempting to sincerely simulate the situation.

Don't get me wrong. This man was not being dishonest. He actually was trying to get at the root of his problem. He really believed he was demon possessed. But in reality he was psychologically disturbed, primarily because of extensive guilt over sin in his life. The meeting he had been in accentuated his guilt so severely that he actually felt he was being attacked by a demon.

The conclusion is obvious. Had we left this young man in a state of turmoil, believing he had a demon that could not be cast out, there's no telling what may have happened to him. This experience left an indelible impression on my mind as to how important it is to differentiate between problems that are psychological and spiritual in origin and those that are not. It is dangerous to dabble in demonism, including attempting to exorcise or contact them. This experience also shows why it was important to have more than one individual involved in this process. If it had not been so, we could have done more harm than good in trying to restore this young man.

What if a person does not respond?

Some don't. I have in my file a letter I sent to a man who had left his wife and family for another woman. However, the letter is *my* letter—unanswered. I sent it to him, following a lengthy talk in which I pleaded with him in gentleness and love to turn from his sin. He was cordial, but unresponsive. I then followed up my confrontation with a personal letter. The letter was returned unopened. I thought it was a mistake and re-sent the letter. Several days later, it was returned again unopened and signed on the outside of the letter by the person I had written. In other words, he was letting me know he did not want to hear from me—and to make the point, he would not even read my letter.

Some people don't respond immediately, but do so later. I have another letter in my file from a Christian I once roomed with before both of us were married. He was an unusually difficult person to get along with. Most everyone he associated with agreed. And, being his roommate, I *really* agreed!

After tolerating his self-centered and abrasive behavior for nearly a year, on one occasion I confronted him with his unspiritual attitudes and actions. With tears streaming down my face, I poured out my frustration. But in the process he sensed I cared. Though he said little after that, his behavior changed. Several years later I received a letter acknowledging that almost everything I had said was true. "I knew it was true," he said, "but I couldn't acknowledge it because of my own pride! I just want you to know, Gene, that I've grown up in that area of my life."

Needless to say, I was not a perfect specimen of spirituality at the time I confronted him. In fact, I was far from it! But God used my sincere attempt to communicate that my reason for confrontation was that I truly loved him and that's why I was vulnerable.

There are those, however, who respond immediately. On another occasion, a young man called me one Sunday after noon. He was very angry with me, with the elders of the church, and with the professors at the seminary where I taught. He also mentioned a few other people in Dallas at whom he was angry. I suggested we get together and talk about his problem. The next day we met in my office.

I discovered that he was really angry with himself. He had lost his job. His wife was threatening to leave him and his family was falling apart.

After a lengthy conversation, and good communication, I suggested that he could have saved me a good deal of pain, as well as himself, if he had called me and acknowledged his frustration and anger—and why. I'll never forget his response. Looking up with tear-stained cheeks, he said, "I know, but you're the first person who has ever loved me enough to tell me what's wrong with me."

As I think back, probably about 50 percent of the people I've tried to restore have responded positively. But, out of them all, I can think of one or two who would have made it all worthwhile. Though the process is often extremely painful, the results are intensely rewarding.

Remember too that some people don't respond because we wait too long. The person may have become so entrenched in his sin that it is very difficult for him to break away from his problem.

Confrontation is the true test of servanthood. It is exciting to serve others when they respond and reciprocate. It's difficult when response is minimal or even negative. But if we are to truly "serve one another in love" in all situations, we should attempt to restore our brothers and sisters who are caught in sin.

Why don't Christians carry out this divine directive stated so clearly by Paul?

There are several reasons. Many of us have not understood our responsibilities. But there are other more basic reasons. First, it's terribly *time-consuming.* And there are so many people who are just waiting to grow spiritually. Yet, we can spend all of our time with problem people. Perhaps if more Christians got involved in the process of restoration, we wouldn't have to neglect the people who want to grow.

Second, it's a *very emotionally draining experience.* Confrontation is difficult. It's enervating. And when there's no response, it's discouraging and threatening. Again, spiritually mature people need to share this burden.

Third, it often involves *rejection.* No one enjoys being rejected. I know I don't. I don't mind the time; I don't mind giving of myself. My greatest struggle is fear of rejection. But then I must remind myself that "perfect love casts out fear" (1 John 4:18, NASB). And the true test of serving one another in love—with "tough love"—is confrontation for restoration.

Fourth, most Christians feel unworthy of this task. We're afraid that the person we confront will point out a weakness in our own lives. This is understandable, but it should not thwart our efforts to restore a person who is caught in some sin. We should, of course, deal with our own weaknesses as much as possible before attempting to restore someone else. More importantly though we must approach the individual in a spirit of humility.

A Challenge

Do you know someone who needs to be restored? Prayerfully consider the guidelines outlined by Paul and reach out to that person in love. If necessary, seek out a couple of other mature Christians who can assist you.

6

Serving One Another—and the "Bottom Line"

The Apostle Paul now turns his thoughts to another significant area of serving—*the use of our material possessions.* In our culture today, and in most cultures of the world, this refers to how we use our money.

The phrase *bottom line* represents a play on words which has been popularized in recent years. It originated in the world of finances. Every business executive is interested in the bottom line. Is the company making a profit or experiencing a loss? When I give a financial report to the elders of our church each month or to the board members of the Center for Church Renewal, they're always interested in the bottom line. Are we in the "red" or the "black"?

But this phrase is often used to describe the *essence* of something. Consequently, in our conversations we often press the question, "What is the bottom line?" In other words, what does all of this mean? What is the main point?

When all is said and done, what is the final conclusion?

In the next portion of the Galatian letter, Paul writes:

> Each one should test his own actions. Then he can take pride in himself, without comparing himself to somebody else, for each one should carry his own load. Anyone who receives instruction in the Word must share all good things with his instructor (Gal. 6:4-6).

In this passage of Scripture, the phrase *bottom line* has both meanings. Paul is dealing with our use of money. But he is also dealing with that which is at the essence of our spiritual life—in many respects, the degree to which we are committed to Christ.

Paul's Basic Exhortation

In Galatians 6:6 Paul captures in one simple statement a basic principle for Christian giving. "Anyone who receives instruction in the Word *must* share all good things with his instructor." Paul is saying that these Galatian Christians should make sure they care for the material needs of their spiritual leaders, especially those who teach them and build them up spiritually.

Paul spoke to this same issue in his first letter to Timothy, but in more specific terms. Timothy was in Ephesus, helping to establish the church. Part of his responsibility was to appoint local leadership. Paul wrote, "The elders who direct the affairs of the church well are worthy of *double honor,* especially those whose work is preaching and teaching" (1 Tim. 5:17).

The phrase *double honor* is a monetary term in the Greek text. In fact, Paul makes this point even clearer in the next verse when he quotes the Old Testament as well as Jesus. "For the Scripture says, 'Do not muzzle the ox while it is treading out the grain,' and 'The worker deserves his wages' " (v. 18).

AN OLD TESTAMENT GUIDELINE. God established this priority in Israel when He revealed the law at Mount Sinai. The Levites were to be set aside as spiritual leaders, and the rest of Israel was to give 10 percent or a "tithe" of their material possessions to care for these men and their families. The Levites in turn were to give 10 percent of what they received to the priests, who were especially appointed to represent Israel before God (Lev. 27:30-33).

In addition, the Jews were commanded by God to give a *second tithe* each year to be used for a sacred meal in Jerusalem (Deut. 12:5-6, 18)—a time of celebration and worship. And every *third year* they were to give a *third tithe,* not only to make sure the Levites were cared for properly, but to meet the needs of widows, orphans, and even the strangers among them—in other words, those in their culture who had no source of income (14:28-29). Thus, every family in Israel was instructed to give, on an average, 22 percent of their yearly income so that the spiritual and social ministry in Israel could be carried on properly.

A NEW TESTAMENT PRINCIPLE. The practice of caring for those who carry on a ministry is clearly reiterated in the New Testament. "Anyone who receives instruction in the Word must share all good things with his instructor" (Gal. 6:6).

Guidelines for Giving

In Galatians 6:4-5, we find at least three guidelines to help us carry out Paul's exhortations in verse 6.

FIRST, EVERY CHRISTIAN SHOULD TEST HIS OWN ACTIONS (6:4a). In our interpretation of this Scripture passage, we often associate verses 4 and 5 with the opening part of this chapter. However, these concepts seem to be contextually related to Paul's exhortation in verse 6. If so, Paul was saying that when it comes to giving, every Christian should test his own actions. We're to evaluate our program of giving in light of God's Word. Are we doing the will of God? Are we keeping "in step with the Spirit" (5:25) in our use of our material possessions? Or are we indulging the sinful nature in this important area of life—reflecting "selfish ambition"? (v. 20)

SECOND, A CHRISTIAN SHOULD NOT COMPARE HIMSELF WITH OTHER CHRISTIANS (6:4b). This is a temptation. Those who cannot give a lot tend to be intimidated by those who can. And sometimes those who can give a lot are tempted to expect more from those who can't give as much as they do.

Thus, Paul seems to be saying, "When it comes to giving, don't compare yourself with others—particularly in terms of amount." Paul also wrote to the Corinthians, *"Each one of you* should set aside a sum of money *in keeping with his income"* (1 Cor. 16:2).

Each of these Christians was to give as God had prospered him. In our culture, a Christian who makes $100,000 a year will be able to give far more proportionately—and should—than a Christian who earns $20,000 a year.

Consequently, Christians should not compare themselves with others in terms of *quantity* of giving. Rather, each of us should test his own actions. Are we giving regularly and proportionately in relationship to *our* particular income? If we are, Paul was saying we will "feel good about ourselves";

that is, we can take pride in ourselves—not in a selfish way, but in a spiritual sense (James 1:9-10).

THIRD, EVERY CHRISTIAN SHOULD CARRY HIS OWN LOAD (Gal. 6:5). This is Paul's third guideline and sets the stage for his exhortation in verse 6. *Every* believer was to do his part. In Paul's thinking, no Christian was exempt—unless, of course, he had no source of income.

It's unfortunate that in the average Bible-believing church, the financial burden of the church is carried by a relatively small percentage of people. There are those who with every degree of regularity give 10 percent or more of their income. Their checks to the church are as regular as their own paychecks. However, statistics show that the great proportion of church attenders are the "cash" givers. Their offerings tend to be what is in their billfold or purse on a given Sunday.

I can identify with this category. When I first became a Christian, I was a cash giver. I gave what I happened to have in my billfold whenever the offering was taken. And since I never carried a lot of cash, and what I had was usually designated for other needs, my giving was very minimal when compared with my income.

I did not become a proportionate giver until I married my wife, Elaine. She taught me both by example and precept what the Scriptures say on this subject. Since we were both living under God's grace rather than His laws, we felt the least we should do would be to give a "first tithe."

It was difficult at first to give in this way, especially since we were just establishing a home. But we decided to live within our 90 percent—and since that day we have never dropped below 10 percent in our giving. It doesn't take a CPA to figure out that if every Christian were a cash giver, there would not be enough money to pay salaries and care for the other needs of the church. The proportionate givers bear this burden. And Paul was saying this should not be. *Every Christian* should carry his own load. And at this juncture, Paul made his main point. "Anyone who receives instruction in the Word *must* share all good things with his instructor" (v. 6).

It's interesting that in the Old Testament, a tithe or 10 percent was designated to care for the needs of those who carried on the spiritual ministry. The other tithes were used to meet the additional needs in Israel.

What would happen if every Christian gave in this way? Let me illustrate. On one occasion I met with a Dallas pastor who informed me that his church added a full-time staff person every time 10 to 12 new families joined the congregation.

"How can this be?" I asked. "It's simple," he responded. "If 10 families give 10 percent, you have a full-time salary. Even if the economic levels vary in each family, 10 "tithes" make up 100 percent—*an average* salary." Frankly, I had never thought of it that way.

I'm not suggesting that a church add a full-time person to the staff every time you add 10 new families. But if every Christian gave 10 percent of his income, it would be possible. And if we gave as they did in Israel—beyond the tithe—we would have all we need to do everything necessary to carry on God's work—in our community and around the world.

The Results of Obedience

What happens when Christians serve one another in this way? We've already illustrated what happens in being able to do God's work. But what are the results in our own lives?

Paul immediately spoke to this point. "Do not be deceived," he wrote. "God cannot be mocked. A man reaps what he sows" (6:7).

Paul also uses this terminology in his second letter to the Corinthians. "Remember this: whoever *sows* sparingly, will also reap sparingly, and whoever *sows* generously will also reap generously" (2 Cor. 9:6).

Does this mean God will reward us financially if we give regularly? It is clear that He made this promise to Israel. Look at these words from Malachi:

> "Bring the whole tithe into the storehouse, that there may be food in My house. Test Me in this," says the Lord Almighty, "and see if I will not throw open the floodgates of heaven and pour out so much blessing that you will not have room enough for it. I will prevent pests from devouring your crops, and the vines in your fields will not cast their fruit," says the Lord Almighty (Mal. 3:10-11).

I believe that "prosperity giving" as it is presented by many TV preachers and local church pastors is not biblical. It is based on carnal and selfish motivation. These leaders tell us, "If you want to get rich, give to the Lord and His work." Personally, I do not believe that the New Testament promises that God is obligated to bless us financially if we give regularly. This was a special promise to Israel as a nation and for a special purpose.

What *will* happen if we give to the Lord? Paul answered this question in 2 Corinthians 9:8-11.

First, God has promised to meet our *needs*—not our wants (v. 8).

Second, He has promised to "enlarge the harvest of your

righteousness" (v. 10). In other words, He will bless us spiritually (Phil. 4:17).

Third, as we give faithfully He has promised to make it possible for us to continue to give. "You will be made rich in every way so that you can *be generous on every occasion*, and through us your generosity will result in thanksgiving to God" (2 Cor. 9:11).

My heart was particularly moved when a member of our church shared with me one day that he had been reading a book that dealt with *grace giving*. "I tithe regularly," he said. "And every time I have written a check, I write on the check Malachi 3:10. But," he continued, "I've discovered the true meaning about grace giving in the New Testament. My motivation has been wrong."

He went on to say he still tithes regularly, but he no longer writes Malachi 3:10 on his checks. "I now give because I have *already* received," he said with a smile on his face.

This man now shares what he has with the Lord and God's people because of the gift of salvation and the blessing he receives regularly from being a part of the body of Christ. This is indeed the kind of motivation that God wants us to have when we give! Later I thought how great it would be if every Christian wrote John 3:16 on checks that are given for the Lord's work.

But what about material blessings?

Does God ever honor our faithfulness as He did in Israel? In most instances I believe He does, especially if our motives are right. Again and again I've heard people give testimony to this fact. My wife and I have seen it in our own lives.

I was particularly blessed when a man in our church called me on the phone one day. He indicated he had never given much to the church. In fact, he was quite honest about the fact that he had very little desire to give. But, on one occasion, a special need was presented and both he and his wife felt the desire to give $1,000—even though this would cause some financial pressure for him in his relatively small business. So they gave.

It was two months later that he called me. "You're not going to believe this," he responded enthusiastically. "A couple of days ago my wife, for the first time in our lives, entered a special contest sponsored by a Dallas newspaper. And would you believe," he exclaimed, "she won the grand prize!" The amount? One thousand dollars.

Is this a fluke—an accident? I don't believe so. God, in His sovereign will, chose to honor this couple's heart motives. They did not give to receive. They were not testing the Lord. And the Lord in His own mysterious way wanted them to know He noticed what they had done. Furthermore, He wanted to encourage them to become regular givers.

Another thing I've discovered is that God doesn't always reward people monetarily. Another member of our church shared with me one day his own journey in the area of giving. When he was just a new Christian, he was learning what the Bible taught about giving. He and his wife decided they wanted to give at least 10 percent. But shortly after they began the process, the shower in their home broke down. The estimate to get it fixed was $250, the amount of their tithe for that month.

He and his wife prayed about the matter and decided to go ahead and give the $250 as planned, trusting the Lord to take care of a very significant problem and need. In the meantime, they used another bathroom. A short time later the Lord brought a person into their lives who showed them how they could fix the shower for less than $2.50.

God has more than one way to meet our needs and to honor our faithfulness. He doesn't necessarily have to work through cash. In this case, God provided skill that was at least a hundredfold return on what these people had given to the church.

Today this man not only tithes from his personal income, but he also tithes his business profits. In other words, he gives 10 percent of his company's profits to the Lord. And he continues to testify to God's blessing in his life and that of his family.

Some Personal Questions

Would you test your own actions? How do you measure up to God's will in this area of your life?

Do you compare yourself with others in this matter? The Bible teaches that you should measure yourself against the Word of God. Don't be intimidated by those who give more than you do. And don't judge those who give less than you do.

Are you serving others by carrying your part of the load? Or are you allowing others to bear the financial burden in the church?

Are you sharing appropriately with those who are ministering to you in the Word? And, are you making this the basic criteria as to where you share *most* of what you give?

Even as a pastor, I have felt that the first and primary place I should give is to the body of believers that ministers to me and my family. And since I'm salaried by a particular church, it goes without saying that my first and primary responsibility in giving must be to those who have shared with me financially. Consequently, my wife and I have always made it a practice to give at least 10 percent of our paycheck from the church we serve, back to the church. If indeed a local church is a primary source of spiritual strength—and it should be—Paul is teaching all Christians that this should be the primary place we share our material resources. This does not mean, of course, we should not support other worthy Christian organizations. But if we neglect our local church, we are not in harmony with God's will for our giving.

A Counter Question

Since we live under grace, does a Christian *have* to give 10 percent? The answer, of course, is no. God doesn't even *demand* that we live for Him in other aspects of our lives. He asks us to, however. He desires it. He wants our voluntary love.

But when Christians ask me how much they should give, my response is, "Should we not, under grace, give at least the first tithe?" In fact, I was meeting one day with Dr. John Walvoord, president of Dallas Seminary, and he shared with me his personal philosophy. "Since the Children of Israel gave an average of at least 22 percent a year, should we not at least do as much under grace?"

I blinked! At this point in his life it became obvious that he was sharing his own approach to giving. I was not intimidated, nor did I compare myself with him, in a negative sense.

His model became a goal in my life. And we all need models. And one day, hopefully, after the children are through college and marriage ceremonies are paid for, it would really be neat to be able to give at least 22 percent each year. My wife and I look forward to the time when that is possible.

A Final Thought

I experienced a lot of emotional anxiety in researching and preparing this material. As I reflected and introspected, I discovered *why.* Quite honestly, the reason was fear of rejection. And this is not an unusual emotion for a pastor. No subject creates more anxiety in Christians than the subject of giving. That in itself is significant. And when we feel uncomfortable, we sometimes reject not only the message, but the messenger.

Dr. Charles Ryrie in his book, *Balancing the Christian Life,* shares why this happens. He writes:

> One of the most *important evidences of true spirituality* is seldom discussed in books or sermons on the subject.

He is referring to how we use our money. Consequently, he continues:

> Our love for God may be proved by something that is a major part of everyone's life, and that is our use of money. How we use our money demonstrates the reality of our love for God. In some ways it proves our love more conclusively than depth of knowledge, length of prayers, or prominence of service. These things can be feigned, but the use of our possessions shows us up for what we actually are (Moody Press, p. 84).

In other words, Dr. Ryrie is saying that this aspect of serving others is in many respects "the bottom line." It touches us at the very depths of our spiritual lives. It should not surprise us that we become defensive if we're not obedient to God in this area. And it shouldn't surprise me as a pastor if I sense that threat—and perhaps even some rejection. But if I avoid teaching on this subject for that particular reason, I would not be true to my calling. I would indeed be a hypocrite!

7
Servants of All

This past week I had one of those rare privileges to conduct a funeral for a dear Christian lady who lived a full and fruitful life. She was born January 11, 1903, just three years into the 20th century and died at the ripe old age of 80.

Her son and his wife attend our church. Sitting down together a few hours before the funeral, Jimmy shared these beautiful words about his mother, which I incorporated into my funeral message:

"Mom was married to my dad for 51 years," he said. "Dad died 9 years before she did. She became a Christian at an early age.... My mother's main concern was for her family. But she loved *all* people—and loved them the way they were, and not for what she or anyone else thought they should be.... She worked over 25 years in the public school lunchroom and she *loved* kids—and they loved her!... She was so giving! Mom shared with others what she had when she knew of a need. She continually gave of herself."

Edna Mae Smith exemplified Paul's words to the Galatian Christians. "Therefore, as we have opportunity, let us do good to all people, especially to those who belong to the family of believers" (Gal. 6:10). As Christians, we are to be "servants of all." All of those who knew Mrs. Smith witnessed this reality in her life.

Doing Good

In this verse Paul definitely prioritizes our serving responsibilities. Our fellow Christians are to be our first concern, but we should be servants to non-Christians as well.

As so often happens when I am in the process of preparing a message, the Lord challenges the very area of my own life that I'm studying about in Scripture. I have a favorite place where I go to work on my messages. Strange as it may seem, I'm able to concentrate best in a restaurant though there are people all around me. I was in this restaurant working on this material. There is one waitress, however, who always seems to make me feel she'd rather I'd not be there. I thought perhaps she was upset with me because I was taking space away from her potential customers, though I've tried to be sensitive to that factor. For example, a week before I had tipped her at least three times the normal amount just to express my appreciation for being able to spend some extra time in her serving station. And just to make sure she *really* knew I appreciated it, I handed her the tip on the way out and thanked her for allowing me to spend so much time there.

Her response jolted me. There was not so much as a "thank you." Frankly, I was perturbed. But Elaine, who was with me, reminded me that perhaps the waitress was embarrassed or just had difficulty expressing herself. So I gave her the benefit of the doubt.

But on this particular day, I walked in and got the same cold response. Fortunately, another waitress took care of me.

"What's her problem?" I asked the other waitress, as I explained what I'd been feeling.

"Oh, she's just having a problem with life," the other waitress responded. "It's not you," she reassured me. "She's just a moody person."

Somewhat relieved—and at the same time still feeling a bit of frustration—I decided to face the problem head-on. I left my table, went over to where the waitress was standing, and said, "I have the feeling you don't like me and you'd rather I not be here. What's the problem?" I even reminded her of the triple tip I had given her a few days before to reassure her I appreciated her service.

Needless to say, she was somewhat nonplussed. She quickly assured me I was welcome, and then went about her business serving others. But I noticed that she kept glancing at me out of the corner of her eye, probably wondering what I was going to do next. I noticed, however, she was making an effort at being more friendly with the other customers. I just went about eating my food and working on this message.

I must confess that my initial reaction to this experience was anger. But then I reflected on the matter and the other waitress' interpretation of her problem. I immediately saw the unique connection between the verse of Scripture I was studying at that very moment and the experience I was having with this waitress. It motivated me to see her in a different light—as a person who probably needed a lot of love and acceptance. Frankly, I don't regret confronting her, for I feel I did it in a loving way. And I feel it helped her to understand how she was coming across to other people. But I determined right then and there to try to *serve her* in some way.

At this juncture, I don't know what her problem is. Maybe her husband is a "louse." Maybe she has a retarded child. Maybe she has been disillusioned by some Christian—and resents the fact that I'm studying my Bible in a public place. Maybe she's just selfish and needs to get her mind off herself. Whatever the problem, my Bible teaches me I'm to do good to *all* people—not just those who belong to the family of believers.

Looking for Opportunities

Note that Paul encouraged these Galatian Christians to "do good to all people" as they had *opportunity.* With this statement he was recognizing the fact that all of us operate within the limits of space and time. In reality, there are more valid needs among both Christians and non-Christians in this world than all of us together could ever meet. But there are *unique* situations that come our way that provide us with opportunities to meet needs in special ways.

This past week one of our pastors reported that a woman who attends our "Formerly Married" group shared that another woman in her office and her children lost everything they owned in an apartment fire. In fact, they escaped with only their nightclothes. Moved by this need, we checked out our own church "Love Fund" and found we were already several hundred dollars in the red. But almost simultaneously, we received a call from a young businessman in our church who wanted to give a substantial sum of money to the church because of the way God had blessed him. When we shared the need with him, he wanted part of the money placed in the "Love Fund" to help this needy person.

We investigated the validity and extent of the need, which we always do because we feel we are responsible to be good stewards of God's money. We then wrote out a substantial check from the Fellowship Bible Church—North to help this person. Hopefully our love will reveal to her the love of Christ—and cause her to respond to that love. Interestingly, after making the gift we found out she already was a Christian. However, when we made the gift, our criteria for giving was not determined by whether she was a Christian.

This was an opportunity I believe that God laid before us. Though we cannot and do not give to every person like this, we felt this was *our moment*—our unique opportunity—to help a person in need and to practice this scriptural injunction. Why? The need was mentioned by one of our own people. Though the money was not available immediately, that same day a member of the body voluntarily called and decided to distribute the money among the "General Fund," the "Building Fund," and the "Love Fund." And what is exciting, the gift to the "Love Fund" was substantial enough that we are now in the black, even after the gift was given. There was no question in our minds that God was saying this was our *special opportunity* to do good.

These opportunities, of course, appear regularly *within* the family of God. Paul makes it clear that this is to be a priority. We're to "do good"—"*especially* to those who belong to the family of believers."

On one occasion, the women of the church planned a

special weekend retreat. They wanted everyone to have an opportunity to go. However, not everyone could afford it. One member of our church, knowing about this "opportunity to do good," voluntarily provided seven scholarships for women who could not afford the cost.

Opportunities to do good, of course, are far more than financially oriented. In fact, I received a beautiful letter from a lady following my message entitled, "Serving One Another and the Bottom Line." In that message I mentioned that in the average Bible-believing church, a small percentage of the people carry the financial burden of the church. She wrote to say that she was one of those who did not support the church substantially. However, she wanted me to know why.

> I want to tell you how I long to give financial support . . . but my situation is an unbelieving spouse. There are many points we differ on and contributing to the church is probably the biggest. We are light-years away on this important principle. I don't fit into the category of poor and needy, nor do I fit into the category of spiritual immaturity, nor do I lack motivation or desire to contribute—I am restrained in obedience to my spouse. Each time I hear a message such as the one God had you deliver Sunday, my heart's desire is to give without measure, but all too soon I'm reminded of the reality of my boundaries. This always brings forth the area of submission to me. Which is more important? I have to "rest" in submission. Resting in submission requires a great deal of patience and endurance.

> I first saw this becoming a pattern in my life about 10 years ago when I gave Him my most valuable asset—my time. Realizing I was being kept back in check as to my giving, I made myself available to God.
>
> Do pray for my husband as he is coming closer and closer to the Lord. My children are both saved and I can't think of anything more perfect than his salvation also.

This letter was a great encouragement to me. Biblically this woman has made the right decision. And until that day when her husband experiences the greatest gift of all, which will indeed unlock his heart to be able to share of what he has with others, she is giving what she has—her time, and she's able to do it in many, many ways.

Opportunities to do good abound. Peter reminds us that doing good is a primary means of revealing the love of God to the unbelieving world.

> Dear friends, I urge you, as aliens and strangers in the world, to abstain from sinful desires, which war against your soul. Live such *good lives* among the pagans that, though they accuse you of doing wrong, they may see your *good deeds* and glorify God on the day He visits us. Submit yourselves for the Lord's sake to every authority instituted among men: whether to the king, as the supreme authority, or to governors, who are sent by him to punish those who do wrong and to commend those who do right. For it is God's will that by *doing good* you should silence the ignorant talk of foolish men.

> Live as free men, but do not use your freedom as a cover-up for evil; *live as servants of God* (1 Peter 2:11-16).

Persevering

As Christians, we sometimes become discouraged in reaching out to others and helping them, particularly when we do not sense significant responses. Paul exhorted, "Let us not become weary in doing good, for at the proper time we will reap a harvest if we do not give up" (Gal. 6:9).

I remember one situation where I was attempting to reach out to a particular individual. Twice we were to meet for lunch and on both occasions the person didn't keep the appointment. Each time, however, I wrote a note expressing my love and availability—and continued to write notes periodically.

On one occasion I called this person's home and his wife answered. I asked her how things were going. She broke down and cried. She told me how badly her husband felt about missing the luncheons, but explained he just couldn't bring himself to face his difficulties with someone else. She also said, "Gene, you'll never know how much your notes have meant to him. Please don't get discouraged! Just keep making contact."

I did, and eventually he responded. He initiated a luncheon, apologized for not responding before, and expressed deep appreciation for my continuing to reach out to him even though he felt incapable of responding. What an exciting culmination! And how encouraging it was when he shared his new commitment to the Lord Jesus Christ.

The "harvest" may come in many ways. It often comes in

this life and it will definitely come in eternity. God is faithful! And Paul encourages us to be faithful too.

Some Personal Questions

Am I *committed* to doing good to *all* people?

This is where we must start. In fact, we must be committed to *doing good* before we will ever touch others' lives in positive ways. But we should realize, of course, that we cannot literally serve "all" people. Rather, we must not allow "favoritism" to take over in our lives (James 2:1-4).

Am I using the unique opportunities to do good that God sends my way?

On occasions these opportunities come in strange and unexpected ways. One day in the church office a man was servicing our copy machine. However, he did not want to complete the task properly before leaving for the day. The facts are we had been having difficulty getting the machine serviced. One of our secretaries asked him to complete the task because of her own previous difficulties in getting service. Furthermore, we needed the machine.

The serviceman finally consented, but not until he had become very rude—so much so that the secretary walked out of the room to avoid any further confrontation.

I happened to come out of my office and overheard her sharing the experience with several others. Frankly, I was very disturbed since I knew instinctively that the serviceman had not been mistreated. Furthermore, it upsets me when one of our staff is improperly treated by *anyone.*

I immediately walked down the hall to the office where the repairman was reluctantly finishing the job. But as I walked, I had time to think about how to approach him,

Initially, I was going to inform him that I was calling his boss right there and then to report his irresponsible behavior.

However, by the time I arrived on the scene, I was able to achieve a degree of objectivity and to develop a spiritual perspective on how to handle this problem.

"Excuse me," I said, "but I need to talk to you about something. You've offended one of our employees and I want you to know that she is a very experienced, professional person who doesn't get upset without a serious reason."

I had his attention!

"Now," I continued, "I don't want to have to call your boss and report this situation as well as the previous problems we've had with your service. We want to establish a good relationship with you. Frankly, I believe you owe our secretary an apology. That's where I think we ought to begin. Don't you agree?"

His behavior initially was a bit defensive, but very quickly his whole attitude and behavior began to change. "Yes," he said, "I had planned to apologize"—and he did. And the next day he was back to do some additional work—and was all smiles and very courteous. Hopefully, we were able to use this opportunity both to confront something that was wrong and at the same time to win a friend—maybe ultimately to win a man to Jesus Christ.

We must be careful not to allow ourselves to respond to non-Christians in inappropriate ways. We dare not "lower" our own attitudes and actions to conform to theirs when they are not what they should be. We are the ones who are responsible to rise above even unjust behavior.

> Am I persevering—not becoming weary in doing good?

Persevering with Christian attitudes is sometimes difficult—particularly in a worldly setting—and when you feel you are being unjustly treated. Several years ago I wrote a letter to a well-known car dealer in Dallas commending both the manager of his body shop as well as the service department personnel for their consistent courtesy and the quality of their work. In fact, the owner was so impressed with the letter that he sent it on to the body shop manager who framed it and hung it in his office. Ever since then, I have received royal treatment when I've entered that particular office.

Several months ago I entered a process that created a great deal of anxiety for me. First, I had to take my car back to the same service department five times before it was finally fixed. The inconvenience was very frustrating. However, I tried to maintain a proper attitude through the whole ordeal.

When I picked the car up the final time, my wife somewhat reluctantly took her car there for service. That night the service department called with an incredible estimate. I couldn't believe it because the car was simply scheduled for a standard checkup.

By this time my trust was so low in the organization that I told Elaine to have them release her car. We took it to another place. Later that day the shop manager from the second place called and said with a chuckle in his voice, "I fixed everything on this car I can find that needs to be fixed and the bill is now a third of the original estimate."

In the meantime, I needed some bodywork done on my car. I took it back to the original body shop—and there on the wall hung the letter I had written three years before. I later picked up the car, having received the same poor quality treatment as before. I explained to the body shop manager I was going to write another letter to the owner, still commending the body shop, but giving an extensive report on the deterioration I had experienced in their service department.

The body shop manager listened intently to my story and then said, "Don't write to 'Mr. So-and-so.' He died two months ago!"

The lights went on in my head, especially when he explained their own concern about what was happening in the service department since the owner's death. He then gave me the name of the new owner who was scheduled to take over. "Write to him," he said. "We're all concerned about correcting the problem."

I share this story because I was on the verge of writing a letter that could have reflected some attitudes that may have been improper. The manager's perspective on the problem changed my perspective—and my feelings. Perhaps now I can *do some good* and maintain a Christian witness. Who knows? Maybe I'll even take my car there for service again someday—something I had determined *never* to do again.

As Christians, we certainly shouldn't let people "walk all over us." But the Bible is clear that there is a way to respond to our unjust treatment—particularly when it involves non-Christians. We are to be servants of all.

8
Servant Leaders

Ever since the dawn of world history, leaders have emerged to direct the affairs of society. Though their motives and style of influence have varied, the great majority have been *self*-serving. Their basic motivation has been power, prestige, and wealth. Jesus alluded to this fact when He referred to the behavior of the "kings of the Gentiles" in Luke's Gospel (Luke 22:25-26).

Unfortunately, the religious community has also had more than its share of egocentric and power-hungry people who manipulate and control others for their own benefit. And it is indeed unfortunate when this mentality becomes evident in the evangelical Bible-believing community.

The Pharisees—A Negative Example

When Jesus began His public ministry in Israel, He found Himself surrounded by a body of religious leaders identified as Pharisees. They were a very legalistic group, intensely zealous for the law. For about a century and a half, they held a position in Israel that *demanded* the highest respect.

The Apostle Paul, before he became a Christian, belonged to this religious group. Writing about his preconversion days in his letter to the Philippians, he reminisced:

> If anyone else thinks he has reason to put confidence in the flesh, I have more: circumcised on the eighth day, of the people of Israel, of the tribe of Benjamin, a Hebrew of Hebrews; in regard to the law, *a Pharisee*; as for zeal, persecuting the church; as for legalistic righteousness, faultless (Phil. 3:4b-6).

Pharisaical leaders like Paul were the object of some of Christ's sharpest, verbal barbs. John Lange, commenting on this fact, wrote:

> It is certainly remarkable that the severest language which Christ ever used, was directed, not against the people, of whom He rather spoke with pity and compassion, nor against the Sadducees, with whom He came less in contact, but against the orthodox, priestly, sanctimonious, hypocritical Pharisees, the leaders of the hierarchy, and rulers of the people (*Commentary on the Holy Scriptures*, Matthew—Luke, Zondervan, p. 409).

CHRIST'S INDICTMENT (Matt. 23:1-7, 13-36). This observation is dramatically illustrated in Matthew 23. Notice some of the direct statements Christ made to these men in the presence of a larger company of onlookers:

> Woe to you, teachers of the law and Pharisees, you hypocrites! (vv. 13, 15, 23, 25, 27, 29)

> Woe to you, blind guides! . . . You blind fools! . . . You blind men! (vv. 16-17, 19)
>
> You snakes! You brood of vipers! (v. 33)

There is no question that Jesus was *very* disturbed with the lifestyle and the leadership style of these leaders in Israel.

Why these strong, negative descriptions? Jesus clearly spelled out His reasons. He said:

> You travel over land and sea to win a single convert, and when he becomes one, you make him twice as much a son of hell as you are (v. 15).
>
> You give a tenth of your spices—mint, dill, and cummin. But you have neglected the more important matters of the law—justice, mercy, and faithfulness. You should have practiced the latter, without neglecting the former (v. 23).
>
> You clean the outside of the cup and dish, but inside they are full of greed and self-indulgence (v. 25).
>
> You are like whitewashed tombs, which look beautiful on the outside but on the inside are full of dead men's bones and everything unclean (v. 27).

Believe it or not, Jesus was directing His words at the *spiritual* leaders in Israel. These men insisted that they be called "rabbi," "master," "father," and "teacher." Their disciples or learners were to follow strict rules in their relationship with these men. For example, they were to follow "without question." In other words, the disciples of the Pharisees dare not allow themselves to assume that these men could be wrong in any respect. They were to afford any given Pharisee the highest possible honor. This, of course, came in many forms. For example, they were never to walk beside their teacher, for this would indicate some kind of equality.

Speaking to the multitudes, Jesus said these men "do not practice what they preach" (v. 3). Furthermore, "everything they do is done for men to see" (v. 5). Thus, Matthew records five times that Jesus identified these so-called "spiritual leaders" as hypocrites.

CHRIST'S LESSON IN LEADERSHIP (Matt. 23:8-12). It is in this context that Jesus addressed His own disciples. Though the context implies it may have involved "the crowds" (v. 1), some commentators believe that He was speaking at this moment to the 12 men He had chosen to follow Him. This seems to be a logical interpretation in view of the fact that He was preparing these men for leadership in what was soon to become a growing Christian community. In many respects this new religious community would be a counterculture to Judaism. Certainly it would introduce to Israel and the pagan world a whole new style of leadership—one characterized by servanthood.

Against this backdrop and recognizing that Jesus was speaking to His 12 men, we can understand more clearly His words in Matthew 23:8-12.

> But you are not to be called "Rabbi," for you have only one Master and you are all brothers. And do not call anyone on earth "father," for you have one Father, and He is in heaven. Nor are you to be

called "teacher," for you have one Teacher, the Christ (vv. 8-10).

It was at this juncture that Jesus made His point. "The greatest among you will be your *servant.* For whoever exalts himself will be humbled, and whoever humbles himself will be exalted" (vv. 11-12).

Some Christians have interpreted Christ's commands to mean it is wrong to use any title for a spiritual leader other than "brother." If this were true, we would have a very difficult time explaining why Christ later identified His men as apostles. Furthermore, the rest of the New Testament uses such titles as apostles, prophets, evangelists, pastors, teachers, elders, bishops, and deacons. In fact, the Apostle Paul identified himself as the Corinthians' "*father* through the Gospel." And in the same context he referred to Timothy as his spiritual son (1 Cor. 4:15, 17). The Apostle Peter also identified Mark in the same way (1 Peter 5:13).

It is virtually impossible to direct an organization without some kind of nomenclature to describe various leadership roles—including churches. Wherever you have function, you have form and structure. And part of that function and form includes leadership roles. This is why elders and deacons were appointed when churches were established in the New Testament culture. You cannot have "leaderless" groups. It is true that Christ is the head of the church, the Chief Shepherd. But He has ordained that human shepherds care for His sheep and direct and manage the affairs of the church.

What then does Jesus really mean in this passage? It's clear from the overall context of Scripture that the Lord is not prohibiting the use of titles per se, but He is dealing with the specific behavior of the Pharisees that was characterized by arrogance, pride, selfish ambition, and horrible abuse of their leadership positions. They were using their titles to demand subservience.

Jesus was also saying that anyone who wants to be a leader in the kingdom of God must first be willing to be a servant. In fact, he *must* be a servant—a servant leader. He must be willing to focus, not on himself and his own needs, but on the needs of others. He must not vie for power, respect, and esteem, but be willing to become one who humbles himself before God and those he serves. And furthermore, Jesus is saying that if any leader in the church today uses titles—even biblically legitimate titles—to *demand* subservience, he is guilty of the same sin as the Pharisees.

Jesus Christ—His Positive Example

A short time later Jesus illustrated what He had been saying to the Pharisees in the presence of His 12 men. Though they were listening that day as Christ pronounced judgment on the Pharisees, they were probably so caught up in the message *to the Pharisees* that they completely missed the fact that the message was primarily *to them.*

This fact was dramatically illustrated shortly before Jesus was crucified. It was time for the Passover meal and Jesus sent two of His disciples into Jerusalem to prepare for the meal. Later, Jesus and the rest of His men arrived and ascended to a large Upper Room. When they entered, preparation had already been made and they reclined at the table to share the meal together.

However, something very interesting happened. In the middle of the meal, Jesus stood up, poured water into a basin, and began to wash the disciples' feet. This was a strange event because it was customary in this culture to wash feet *before* a meal—not in the *middle* of the meal.

What had happened? When Jesus and the 12 men arrived, they walked into the room. Knowing their attitudes and inner struggles, they first of all rushed about to see who could find the best place at the table, particularly so they might be next to Jesus.

Second, they completely ignored the basin of water and towel that had been provided. In their culture, people walked on dirty, contaminated roads and streets, either barefoot or in sandals. It was just as customary to "wash feet" before eating as it is to "wash our hands" in our 20th-century American culture.

But not one of the disciples volunteered to be the servant in this situation. It appears that Jesus purposely and patiently waited to see if one of those rascals would take the initiative. Not one did! So Jesus, in the middle of the meal, personally volunteered to be that servant.

This explains Peter's embarrassment and his initial refusal to allow Jesus to wash his feet. He understood clearly the message Jesus was conveying. He was ashamed that he had not taken the initiative when they first arrived.

What Jesus was teaching these men that day was coming through loud and clear. They had been arguing among themselves over who was to be the greatest in Christ's kingdom, even during the Passover meal (Luke 22:24). Perhaps it was at this moment that Jesus quietly rose and began the process of washing their feet.

When He finished this task, He made His point, beginning with a question:

"Do you understand what I've done for you?" He

> asked them. "You call me a 'Teacher' and 'Lord,' and rightly so, for that is what I am. Now that I, your Lord and Teacher, have washed your feet, you also should wash one another's feet. I have set you an example that you should do as I have done for you" (John 13:12b-15).

Luke gives us some additional insights, not only regarding what Jesus did and said, but regarding what was happening in the hearts of these men. Describing the scene while they were eating the meal, he wrote:

> Also a dispute arose among them as to which of them was considered to be greatest. Jesus said to them, "The kings of the Gentiles lord it over them; and those who exercise authority over them call themselves benefactors. But you are not to be like that. Instead, the greatest among you should be like the youngest, and the one who rules like the one who serves. For who is greater, the one who is at the table or the one who serves? Is it not the one who is at the table? But I am among you as one who serves" (Luke 22:24-27).

God's Leadership Plan for the Christian Community

All along Jesus was setting the stage for what He wished to happen in the Christian community after He returned to heaven. The apostles, under the leadership of the Holy Spirit, would be His human representatives to launch that great movement we call the church. And once local churches were launched, the apostles were to appoint spiritual leaders to direct the affairs of each church.

SERVANT LEADERS IN THE CHURCH. The Scriptures identify the primary leaders in these churches as elders or bishops. These words were used interchangeably in the New Testament culture.

The Apostle Peter, when writing to a group of churches many years later, revealed how well he had learned the lesson Jesus had taught that day in the Upper Room. Thus, he wrote emphasizing the *servant* aspects of this leadership role. "Be shepherds of God's flock that is under your care," he wrote, "*serving* as overseers—not because you must, but because you are willing." He warned them against being "greedy for money," and exhorted these men to be "eager to *serve;* not lording it over those entrusted to you." And just as Christ was Peter's servant example that day in the Upper Room, the elders were also to be servant examples "to the flock" (1 Peter 5:2-3).

As an elder and pastor over the years, I've had the privilege to serve with men who have served as fellow elders. At the present time, I serve with six men whom I believe exemplify servant leader qualities in unusual ways. They are all models to me and their lives are constant reminders that I am to be, by God's design, a servant leader. True, we are to lead the church. We are to manage well (1 Tim. 3:5). That is our responsibility, but with only one purpose in mind—to *serve* the body of Christians entrusted to our care. We are to be servant leaders. Every decision, every action on our part should be for the benefit of those we serve and for the honor and glory of Jesus Christ.

SERVANT LEADERS IN THE HOME. The family is an even more basic social unit in the Christian community. In fact, the Bible functionally defines the Christian home as the "church in miniature." And God's ordained leaders in the family function through two primary roles—husband and father. As a Christian husband, I am to love my wife as "Christ loved the church and gave Himself up for her" (Eph. 5:25). As a father, I am not to "embitter" or "exasperate" my children, but I am to "bring them up in the training and instruction of the Lord" (Col. 3:21; Eph. 6:4). Following Paul's example as a spiritual father, I am to deal with my own children one by one, "encouraging, comforting and urging [them] to live lives worthy of God" (1 Thes. 2:12).

Jesus Christ, who was God in the flesh, has demonstrated with His own life that it is possible to be a servant leader. This is not a contradictory concept. It is uniquely Christian. It is possible to lead strongly and deliberately and to "manage well." But it is possible to do so with humility, compassion, and with a servant's heart.

As I reflect on my own experience as a young person growing up, I could not help but think of my own father. He went to be with the Lord at age 78.

Dad was not an educated man. He was only able to finish the sixth grade. He was not exceptionally intelligent, nor was he the greatest businessman in the world. Toward the end of his life, he often shared with me how he wished he had made certain decisions that would have enhanced the family's financial position. But he was often restricted by fear because of some painful experiences during the Great Depression—primarily, I believe, because his own father made some financial decisions that were disastrous. Consequently, Dad often became so conservative he made decisions in the opposite direction.

But I shall never forget one characteristic that permeated

my dad's life. And to me, it was a far greater gift than material inheritance. He had a servant's heart.

Let me share a personal experience to illustrate this point. When I was six years old, my mother's father came to live in our home. Over the years I discovered Grandpa had a very serious psychological illness. In fact, it wasn't until I took my first college course in psychology that I understood the nature of his illness, what caused it, and why it manifested itself the way it did.

My grandfather was manic-depressive; that is, there were periods in his life when he would be very normal. Then, he would move into a "manic" phase, when he was extremely active and consistently focused on three desires. First, he wanted to get remarried. Second, he wanted to buy a farm. And, third, he wanted to become an active member of the church that my family had belonged to for years. Ironically, these manic periods were also characterized by extreme drinking, foul language, intense expressions of anger, and even physical violence.

Following this manic period, which often lasted at least a year, he would move into a depressive phase. He would stop eating regularly, lose weight, and stay in bed most of the time. It was during this period that he believed that God had forsaken him and that his soul was condemned to eternal hell. He was so depressed he could hardly care for himself. Again, this period would last at least a year.

Then Grandpa would begin to come out of the depressive phase and move into a normal phase. It was during those periods that I remember him as a perfect gentleman. He created no problems around the home, worked about the farm, and was as cooperative as anyone could expect. He was just a loving and kind old man. My fondest memories were to see him gently holding my little sisters as he sat in his old rocking chair.

But then the cycle would eventually start over again. He would move into the manic phase, then into the depressive phase, and finally back into the normal phase. During my grade school and high school years, I saw my grandfather move through at least five of these cycles.

Once I studied this psychological phenomenon in college, I also began to understand why his manic phases manifested certain attitudes and actions. During the Great Depression *he had lost his farm*—which is why during the manic phases he always wanted to once again buy a piece of land. During the same period of time, *his wife died*—which is why he always wanted to remarry. Furthermore, he had been a very immature Christian during this time and he fell into some kind of moral sin after his wife died, but because he was a part of a religious movement that didn't understand grace and forgiveness, he was *excommunicated from the church.* When he cried out for help, in their ignorance and judgmental attitudes, these Christians turned a deaf ear.

As I read and studied about "manic-depressive" illness in college, my mind went back over the years and the picture came into clear focus. I began to understand my grandfather's predicament. We know now, of course, that with modern drugs and proper psychiatric care, followed by proper spiritual counsel, he could have lived a fairly normal life. But in those days no one really understood those problems.

Why do I tell this story? Can you imagine the pressure this put on my family over the years—particularly on my own father? I remember events that were incredible. For example, when Grandfather was in a manic state and wanted to buy a farm, he tried to force my father to loan him money to do so. Dad didn't have the money, and if he had, it would have been irresponsible to allow a sick man to do what my grandfather wanted to do.

Mealtimes were often the most difficult. It was then that Grandpa would make his move on my dad. I remember times when he shouted and cursed my father and beat the table so hard with his fist that plates flew all over the kitchen. But never once during all those years do I remember my dad responding with anger or retaliation. Somehow in his heart, he knew Grandpa was sick and he treated him with unbelievable patience and incredible grace.

One night Grandpa appeared at my parents' bedroom door, threw it open, and walked into their room with a butcher knife in his hand—threatening to kill my father if he didn't loan him the money to buy a farm. I remember so vividly seeing my father get out of bed, slowly walk toward Grandpa, and with a calm and gentle voice, say, "Put it away, Dad," referring to the knife. In a matter of minutes, Grandpa retreated to his room.

Grandpa spent the rest of his days in our home, until he died at age 90. As the years passed, the problem subsided because of his age.

I would never advocate that any family do what my family did. But my mother was the only Christian in my grandpa's family at that time who was married to a Christian man who would even be willing or able to tolerate this situation. Furthermore, because of the lack of psychiatric care, there was no place where his loved ones could put him where they felt he would be cared for properly.

Ironically, I reflect on this experience with gratefulness. As I've talked with my three brothers and two sisters, all of whom went through the same experience, we *now* see it as a positive influence on our lives rather than a negative one. In fact, we can discern no negative scars.

For me personally, Dad's servant heart impacted my own, and I'll never forget his example as long as I live. I frankly do not believe that in a situation like his I would have had the same grace and endurance that he did. But his example has at least encouraged me to be more patient and more of a servant in my own circumstances.

When I compare my own circumstances and opportunities with Dad's, I must conclude that there is no comparison. As I reflect on what I have just shared with you, I have to ask myself a very pointed question. If I had to face the same problems he faced with my grandfather over the same period of time, would I—even with all of my advantages—be able to *serve* as he did? Would I be able to endure it so patiently? I'm not sure I could say yes to that question. Nevertheless, it causes me to thank God even more for my dad's role as a servant leader. I'm convinced when the rewards are given out in heaven, there will be something very special for Dad—something that most of us will never be able to understand or comprehend.

Some Personal Questions

1. What kind of a servant leader am I?
2. As a father or mother, what kind of a servant leader am I in my family?
3. As a husband, what kind of a servant leader am I to my wife?

4. As a member of the body of Christ in my church, what kind of a servant leader am I to others?

9

Servant Teachers

Most of my adult life I have been a teacher. And over the years I've experienced all kinds of reactions to *what* I've taught and to *how* I've taught it. Overall the response has been positive, but on occasions I've encountered some negative reactions. I've had people get up and walk out because they've disagreed with what I've said. I've been publicly accused of being prejudiced. In various academic settings, I've been told I've been unfair in my testing and grading procedures—which in some instances was no doubt true. And I've been openly criticized for teaching certain concepts.

One of my most startling experiences happened when I was teaching overseas in Hong Kong. Twice, a middle-aged man from Great Britain interrupted my teaching sessions and tried to take over the class, accusing me of being a proud and arrogant American Christian who needed to repent of my sins and turn to God. The final time, he not only directed his verbal barbs at me, but marched up and down the aisle of the meeting place and verbally attacked every member of the group.

This experience, of course, was extreme. The man was obviously emotionally disturbed. But how is a Christian teacher to react to those who disagree with him? I must confess that my natural tendency, particularly when I'm attacked publicly, is to react with anger and to use my position of authority to retaliate. No one likes to be embarrassed publicly.

It is clear from Scripture that an intricate, significant part of being a servant leader is being a servant teacher. In fact, it is virtually impossible to be a successful servant leader without being able to apply God's principles of communication.

It is not by chance that the biblical quality used to describe a servant *teacher* is outlined by Paul in the qualifications for eldership. Paul used one word in the New Testament, the Greek word *didaktikos,* but in English it is translated "able to teach" (1 Tim. 3:2).

This word (or phrase) is used only twice in the New Testament. As already stated, it appears initially in Paul's first letter to Timothy in which he outlines the qualifications for eldership. The second time "able to teach" appears is in the second letter to Timothy, but in a much larger context of meaning. It is here that Paul directly relates being "able to teach" to what should characterize a servant leader. After warning Timothy not to "have anything to do with foolish and stupid arguments" (2 Tim. 2:23), Paul wrote:

And the *Lord's servant* must not quarrel; instead,

> he must be kind to everyone, ABLE TO TEACH, not resentful. Those who oppose him he must *gently instruct,* in the hope that God will grant them repentance leading them to a knowledge of the truth (vv. 24-25).

"Able to Teach"—The Basic Proposition

Paul's basic concern in this passage is that Timothy be able to communicate God's truth effectively to those who were untaught regarding God's will. And even more specifically, he was concerned that Timothy be able to teach those who were resistant to knowing and doing the will of God.

Building on his initial warning to avoid arguments, Paul outlined a strategy for Timothy to help him communicate with people who were sincerely searching for truth, but who may not have a correct understanding of God's Word. He included in this category those who may disagree with basic Christian beliefs and opposed Timothy's ministry.

AVOID ARGUMENTS. How do we avoid arguments? Paul first warned Timothy to avoid certain subjects—subjects that are of little value and worth, but which can create heated disagreements.

Earlier in 2 Timothy 2, Paul outlined some of the things he had in mind. First, he warned against *semantic arguments:*

> Warn them before God against *quarreling about words;* it is of no value, and only ruins those who listen (2:14).

Words, of course, are important. We need words to express ourselves and to communicate truth. But some people get so caught up in verbal definitions and rhetoric that they miss the essence of what God is saying.

The Jews were notorious for generating arguments based upon this kind of communication. This is why Paul exhorted Titus to "avoid foolish controversies and genealogies and arguments and quarrels about the law, because these are unprofitable and useless" (Titus 3:9).

Second, Timothy was to avoid arguing about *flagrant false doctrine:*

> Avoid *godless chatter,* because those who indulge in it will become more and more ungodly. Their teaching will spread like gangrene. Among them are Hymenaeus and Philetus, who *have wandered away from the truth.* They say that the resurrection has already taken place, and they destroy the faith of some (2 Tim. 2:16-18).

As Christians, we should certainly be concerned about people who are under the influence of false doctrine. But Paul warned against false teachers who purposely propagate teachings that are out of harmony with the basic doctrines of classical Christianity. For example, most cults and isms deny the deity of Christ. In many respects, this doctrine is at the heart of Christianity, just as the doctrine of the resurrection is. It does no good, Paul said, to argue with these people.

Third, Paul warned Timothy against getting involved in arguments reflecting *immature attitudes and motives:*

> Flee the *evil desires of youth,* and pursue *righteousness, faith, love,* and *peace,* along with those who call on the Lord out of a pure heart" (2:22).

Opposite of what Paul outlined for Timothy to pursue are the "evil desires of youth":

1. Unrighteousness (rather than righteousness)
2. A focus on human reason (rather than faith)

3. Anger, resentment, and bitterness (rather than love)
4. Creating disunity (rather than working toward peace)

BE KIND TO ALL. Paul recognized that it is impossible to avoid situations involving disagreement, especially if we are to be vital witnesses in this world. There are those who are sincerely seeking after truth. They do not disagree just to disagree or to stir up an argument. They have honest questions. How should the Lord's servants respond and deal with these situations? Paul's next three guidelines speak to this question.

The word Paul used for being "kind" (*eepios*) appears only one other time in the New Testament, and then is translated "gentle" in the *New International Version.* However, the way Paul used the word is loaded with meaning. This word appears in Paul's first letter to the Thessalonians in which he described his behavior and that of his fellow missionaries, Timothy and Silas, when they first ministered among these people. "As apostles of Christ we could have been a burden to you, but we were *gentle* among you, like a mother caring for her little children" (1 Thes. 2:7).

Paul's illustration is powerful and very intimate. It describes the process of nurturing these new believers by referring to a mother who is nursing her newborn. There is, of course, no more potent illustration to describe tenderness, gentle caring, and kindness. Thus, Paul is saying that the Lord's servant should relate to immature Christians with the same attitudes and actions. "Be kind to all," he said (2 Tim. 2:24).

Paul is not advocating a "condescending" attitude that conveys the idea, "I'm the parent and you're the child." Rather, he is advocating attitudes and actions that convey gentleness and tenderness and concern in an "adult-to-adult" fashion.

DO NOT BE RESENTFUL. The *New American Standard Bible* translates this concept more meaningfully—be "patient when wronged" (2 Tim. 2:24). It is one thing to be patient when people are responding to truth. It is yet another to be patient when falsely accused, misquoted, and misinterpreted. Using modern terminology, Paul was saying that the Lord's servant should attempt to be "nondefensive" and "nonthreatened" when dealing with people who respond in unkind ways.

Having been a full-time professor most of my life (before becoming a full-time pastor), I can vividly remember situations I have faced in classrooms that I'd rather forget. One incident happened when I was just beginning my teaching career at Moody Bible Institute as a very young professor. In fact, I had one student in a particular class who was several years older than I was.

Shortly after the semester started, he began to give me a rough time—asking tough questions, disagreeing with my answers, and generally creating disunity in the class. Naturally, it was embarrassing for me. In fact, one day I became so frustrated and angry, I dismissed the class in the middle of the session and walked out.

Sometime later, the man appeared in my office, apologized, and asked my forgiveness. In the process he stated why he had given me such a rough time. Unknown to me, he had been interested in dating the girl I had married and he resented the fact that she responded to me rather than to him. His means of retaliation even after I had married Elaine, was to openly disagree with me in the classroom. And since he was some years my senior and in some respects more experienced in life—even as a student—it became a highly threatening situation. Needless to say, I didn't measure up to Paul's strategy for handling this kind of problem. The fact remains I was the teacher, he the student. The burden for handling the matter responsibly remained primarily on my shoulders.

CORRECT WITH GENTLENESS. Paul gave another guideline for handling people who disagree with what you may be teaching. "Those who oppose him [the Lord's servant] he must gently instruct," Paul exhorted Timothy (v. 25). More literally, Paul was saying the Lord's servant must correct a person's thoughts, attitudes, and actions with the spirit of humility and meekness.

In retrospect, of course, I can think of ways I could have handled that situation at Moody Bible Institute more maturely and effectively if I had applied this principle. Hindsight, of course, is always better than foresight. If I had it to do over again, I would have approached the student *privately* after class and have said something like this:

> Bob, (not his real name), I sense there is something between us. Maybe it is how I perceive the situation, but I get the feeling you don't like me, that you're purposely asking questions to embarrass me in front of the class, and then responding with further disagreement. Am I perceiving correctly? Or is there something I'm misreading or misunderstanding?

When I've taken this approach, which I believe is in harmony with what Paul is teaching in this passage, I've found that most people respond positively. And, of course, at times I discover that I am the primary cause of the problem. But the challenge that we face is to be able to apply this principle of correcting with gentleness on a consistent basis.

There are those, of course, who do not respond to gentleness, love, and humility. They are purposely divisive and selfishly motivated. They are totally unteachable and unresponsible. In cases like this, Paul outlines an approach:

> Warn a divisive person once, and then warn him a second time. After that, have nothing to do with him. You may be sure that such a man is warped and sinful; he is self-condemned (Titus 3:10-11).

Here Paul was talking about men like Hymenaeus and Philetus—men who "have wandered away from the truth" (2 Tim. 2:17-18). However, it is clear from a total scriptural perspective that the strategy Paul outlined for Titus should be taken *only* after making every effort to apply the principles outlined for Timothy. Breaking fellowship with a person is always the last resort.

BE TEACHABLE. The word *didaktikos* which is translated "able to teach" comes from a classical Greek word which originally meant "teachable." In other words, this New Testament word, though it means to teach others, has in its historical roots the meaning to "be open to being taught by others." Inherent in the basic concept of being "able to teach" is the idea of also "being teachable."

This is significant and correlates with the principles outlined by Paul. When the Lord's servant avoids arguments and is kind to all, when he is patient when wronged and corrects with gentleness—he is at the same time demonstrating a "teachable spirit" while he is in the process of teaching others. This too is an important part of being a servant teacher. After all, no one has learned all there is to learn. And some of our greatest lessons can come from those we are teaching. In fact, one of my greatest lessons in learning what it really means to be "able to teach" came from my negative experience with that student in the classroom at Moody Bible Institute. Though he eventually apologized for his behavior, I would have been a much better example to the other students had I handled the situation more maturely.

While attending a retreat with a group of church leaders, I heard one of our own elders, Mike Cornwall, share an experience I'll never forget. One Saturday morning while Mike and Sharon were sitting at the breakfast table, a busload of people pulled up at their home. Peering through their kitchen window, to their surprise they saw these people get off the bus, pick up placards, and begin to march up and down the sidewalk in front of their home. It suddenly dawned on Mike and Sharon that these minority people were picketing their premises. Then the leader of the group knocked on the Cornwalls' front door with a document in his hand, demanding that Mike sign it.

Since Mike was a top executive officer with First Texas Savings and Loan, these people had targeted him to demonstrate that his financial organization was unfair to minorities. There stood the leader of this particular group, demanding that Mike sign a document acknowledging the unfairness of their policy. To complicate matters, there stood a photographer, no doubt intending to take a picture of Mike's refusal to sign, which this group would turn over to the press.

What would you have done? The Apostle Paul would have been proud of Mike's response. Rather than allowing himself to be dragged into an argument, he invited these people to come into his home to discuss the matter over a cup of coffee.

You can imagine the look on the leader's face. Somewhat nonplussed, he returned to the group marching up and down the sidewalk. He conveyed Mike's invitation, which again resulted in some consternation. But after a brief discussion, they laid down their placards and one by one marched into Mike's family room. Sharon served them coffee as Mike began to share his experiences in Dallas and what he personally had done and was attempting to do for minorities. At an appropriate moment, he bridged into his personal testimony, explaining how he rather recently had become a Christian and how it had changed his own perspective of life and people.

Little by little, the barriers went down. He even heard a few "Amens" from the group. And after a rather lengthy time of discussion, these people, one by one, got up, thanked the Cornwalls for their hospitality, got back on the bus and left—with the unsigned document—and no pictures.

Mike shared this story at this retreat and afterward, I shared the verses of Scripture we have just studied in this chapter. Frankly, his personal testimony illustrates a 20th-century application of what Paul was teaching Timothy more graphically than any I have personally experienced or encountered. How easy it would have been for Mike to be led into an argument. But instead, he was "kind to *everyone*" and patient when wronged. These people were angry and opposed to what they thought Mike stood for. But rather than becoming defensive, Mike invited them into his home and set about to gently instruct them in a context of love and acceptance. Consequently, he was able to gain a hearing from a group of people who were anything but teachable and very uninformed when they arrived on the scene. This, I believe, is what Paul meant when he wrote, "And the Lord's servant must not quarrel; instead, he must be kind to everyone, able to teach, not resentful. Those who oppose him he must gently instruct, in the hope that God will grant them repentance leading to a knowledge of the truth" (2 Tim. 2:24-25).

Some Personal Questions

Paul's primary focus in his letter to Timothy was, of course, the church. But the principles apply in our relationships with non-Christians and apply particularly in the family. This is especially true since the home is the "church in miniature." As parents, we need to ask ourselves these questions:

1. To what extent am I avoiding arguments and quarrels with my children by applying these principles?
2. Am I responding to their reactions with kindness and gentleness—and to *all* my children in this way?
3. Am I able to respond with patience and non-defensiveness, particularly when I am wronged?
4. Am I able to gently instruct when I have to correct my children? To what extent have I been able to maintain that unique balance between being firm and yet sensitive and gentle?
5. Am I teachable as a parent, realizing that I may not have all the right answers or the right perspective on every situation?
6. In other words, am I "able to teach"? More specifically, am I a servant teacher?

A Final Thought

If a parent can apply these principles effectively in the home, he can probably apply them anywhere. Thus, Paul taught in his first letter to Timothy that if we can manage our own family well, we will also be able to manage the church of God.

10

The Supreme Servant

When Jesus washed the disciples' feet in the Upper Room, He was in actuality illustrating "servanthood" at a level they could understand at that moment in their spiritual pilgrimage. They were far from mature. Their thoughts, intentions, and hopes were intensely self-centered and oriented toward earthly prestige. They were thinking of an earthly kingdom, in which Christ would be the King and they would surround His throne as His top advisers and consultants. In fact, some were already arguing over who would be the greatest in His kingdom (Luke 22:24). Christ thus chose an experience to illustrate servanthood that they could relate to in their immature spiritual state. But with this illustration Christ was pointing to a demonstration of servanthood that was far beyond anything they could grasp at that moment in their lives.

But eventually they *did* understand. Certainly Peter

learned the true meaning of servanthood. Tradition tells us that when he eventually faced martyrdom, he requested to be crucified upside down since he did not feel worthy of being crucified in the same position as the Saviour. And years later, the Apostle John, who in the Upper Room was just as self-centered as the others, wrote about the true meaning of that foot-washing experience. "This is how we know what love is," he said. "Jesus Christ laid down His life for us. And we ought to lay down our lives for our brothers" (1 John 3:16).

We could paraphrase that statement as follows: "This is how we know what true *servanthood* is: Jesus Christ *illustrated* it in the Upper Room when He washed our feet, but He *demonstrated* it when He, the Lord of the universe, chose to walk among all of us and to ultimately give His life that we might have eternal salvation. Therefore we ought to *serve one another* in the same way, even if it means giving our lives for our brothers and sisters in Christ."

The Apostle Paul describes this truth graphically and fully in Philippians 2:1-8. And in this text he exhorts us all to have the same attitude as Christ (v. 5). What was this attitude?

Christ's Example

Paul writes that Jesus, "being in very nature God, did not consider equality with God something to be grasped, but made Himself nothing, taking the very nature of a servant, being made in human likeness. And being found in appearance as a man, He humbled Himself and became obedient to death—even death on a cross!" (Phil. 2:6-8) These words to the Christians in Philippi represent one of the most profound passages in the New Testament. Bible scholars often call it the "Kenosis passage." The word *kenosis* in Greek means "to empty." Paul describes how Christ "emptied Himself" when He became a human being.

These verses could comprise a basis for a whole book. But to get involved in all of the intricacies of the Incarnation could easily interfere with our being able to understand the primary reason Paul was writing about this event—*to demonstrate Christ's servant heart* and how this relates to each of us in the body of Christ. Let's look at the attitudes that Christ demonstrated.

UNSELFISHNESS (v. 6). Christ in His preincarnate state was "very nature God." He experienced an "equality with God" that was not characterized by human dimensions. The Apostle John has written that Christ always existed and "was with God" and "was God." Further, John tells us that "through Him all things were made" (John 1:1, 3).

This is a concept we cannot understand with our finite minds. We can only accept the fact that it is true and recognize that if it were not true, Christianity would be the same as any other religion. It would simply be another religious philosophy that was developed and promoted by a religious leader for selfish reasons. Its source would be earth, not heaven.

But not so with Christianity. Its source was unselfishness personified in Christ Jesus: "who, being in very nature God, did not consider equality with God something to be grasped" (Phil. 2:6). He was willing to give up His *heavenly position* to occupy an *earthly position*—to identify with the very people He had created. Christ's unselfish act of love was and is unequaled in the universe.

HUMILITY (v. 7). Another attitude demonstrated by Jesus

Christ was a willingness to make "Himself nothing, taking the very nature of a *servant*, being made in human likeness" (v. 7). In many respects this is the central focus of this passage.

Does this mean Christ became less than God? Not at all! Rather, He became the God-Man. But He left the glories of heaven to do it. He was born into this world as any other human being, with the exception that His Father was God. He did not come as a king, born to royalty, but as a servant. His first earthly home was a stable surrounded by animals. His parents were peasants, and His first visitors were shepherds. Probably two whole years went by before He made contact with anyone of royal blood, the wise men from the East. What we see in Jesus' birth is the greatest act of humility ever demonstrated.

SACRIFICE (v. 8). To give up the glories of heaven: this is *unselfishness!* To be born as a man: this is *humility!* But to die on a cross for the sins of the world: this is the greatest *sacrifice* known anywhere in the universe. To imitate this attitude is the most significant ingredient in being a servant of Jesus Christ. "Greater love has no one than this," Jesus once said to His disciples, "that one lay down his life for his friends" (John 15:13). Jesus, of course, did lay down His life for His friends—but more so! He died for the sins of the whole world. Thus, He also laid down His life for His enemies.

The disciples did not initially understand the deeper meaning of the foot-washing experience in the Upper Room. But following Christ's death and resurrection, their hearts were opened and they saw the true meaning of being a servant. John states it most clearly, "This is how we know what love is: Jesus Christ laid down His life for us. And we ought to lay down our lives for our brothers" (1 John 3:16).

Paul's Application

Paul had already stated in this passage that our "attitude should be the same as that of Christ Jesus" (Phil. 2:5). But he was even more specific in the verses that precede Christ's example.

"Do nothing out of *selfish* ambition or vain conceit" (v. 3a). Christ, of course, is our supreme example. And as Christ, we are not to be motivated by selfishness. His willingness to lay aside the glories of heaven to be identified with lost humanity demonstrates this quality in the ultimate sense.

"In *humility* consider others better than yourselves" (v. 3b). The basis of unselfishness is humility. Conversely, pride motivates us toward selfishness. And once again, Christ is our model. Consider the fact that He "was with God"! The facts are He "was God"! And yet, Christ was able to view us as objects of grace and love and to humble Himself, in actuality treating us better than Himself. How God could assume this posture is a mystery. But He that was greatest indeed became servant of all.

"Each of you should look not only to your own interests, but also to the *interests of others*" (v. 4). The Bible brings amazing balance to life. It sets a high standard, but it recognizes our human needs. And here is a unique example. Paul demonstrates that each of us has our own personal interests—our mates, our children, our friends, our vocations, etc. And each of us has our own personal needs. To "have the mind of Christ" in no way means we are selfish or proud if we concern ourselves with those interests and needs.

Maintaining the balance is not easy. And keeping our motives proper is even more difficult. But if we follow Christ's example of thinking of others *before* we think of ourselves, we'll find that balance in our lives as we live them day by day, making those important decisions.

Another test of our willingness to be a servant emerges in those situations where to choose our own interests first would violate God's ultimate purposes. Even Christ struggled with this decision when He prayed, "My Father, if it is possible, may this cup be taken from Me. Yet not as I will, but as You will" (Matt. 26:39). Christ went on to pay the ultimate price—death—because to choose another way would violate the will of God.

Few of us are called on to pay the ultimate price in order to serve God and others. But throughout history there are noble examples of this very act of love.

The story is told of George Atley, a young Englishman who was engaged in the Central African mission. He was attacked by a party of natives. He had with him a Winchester repeating rifle with 10 loaded chambers. His attackers were completely at his mercy. He could have destroyed them one by one.

It seems that he calmly and quickly summed up the situation and concluded that if he killed these men it would do the mission and the cause of Christ more harm than if he allowed them to take his own life. So, as a lamb to the slaughter he was led. And when his body was found in the stream, his rifle was also found with its 10 chambers still loaded.

When the *Empress of Ireland* went down with 130 Salvation Army officers on board, 109 officers were drowned. A few survivors told how the people on board, finding there were not enough life preservers for all, took off their own belts and strapped them even on strong men saying, "I can die better than you can"; and from the deck of that sinking ship flung their battle cry around the world.

Jim Elliot was martyred, along with four other men, attempting to reach the Auca Indians in South America. This quotation, taken from his diary, has become a tremendous challenge to all of us as Christians: "He is no fool who gives what he cannot keep to gain what he cannot lose."

Our Motivation

What should motivate a Christian to be a servant of God and others? What can cause us to imitate Christ's attitude?

Paul answered these questions, even before he exhorted the Philippian Christians to follow Christ's servant example.

OUR POSITION IN CHRIST (Phil. 2:1a). Paul made this point before he challenged these believers to follow Christ's example. Your "encouragement," he wrote, should come "from being united with Christ." When we were without hope in this world, Christ made it possible for us to have hope. And that hope came into our lives because of Christ's servant heart toward us. Therefore, our motivation to serve others should come because of God's marvelous grace toward us when we were undeserving sinners. When we are tempted to be selfish and proud, we need to think of what Christ did for us.

CHRIST'S UNCONDITIONAL LOVE (v. 1b). Clearly aligned with our position in Christ is the love of God that places us in the body of Christ and then continues to flow from His heart to us. This is what John had in mind when he wrote, "Dear friends, since God so loved us, we also ought to love one another" (1 John 4:11).

OUR RELATIONSHIP WITH THE HOLY SPIRIT (v. 1c). When we became Christians, Christ came to live in our hearts in the person of the Holy Spirit. Thus each time we become self-serving we are out of harmony, not only with the will of God, but with the very One who resides within us. Everywhere we go, He goes. Everything we do, He is personally present, residing in a heart that is violating what He stands for.

On the other hand, the Holy Spirit desires to assist us in conforming our lives to Christ. It is impossible to live as Christ lived without relying on the Holy Spirit and being in proper fellowship with Him. He is our ultimate source, not only for our motivation to live like Christ, but He is our ultimate strength.

CHRIST'S EXAMPLE OF TENDERNESS AND COMPASSION (v. 1d). On one occasion Jesus Christ looked over Jerusalem and wept (Luke 19:41). His heart was broken because of the hearts of people who had become calloused and hard. Christ exemplified tenderness and compassion. Paul has exhorted all Christians to exemplify the same qualities in their relationships with others. A Christian without tenderness and compassion is a living contradiction to all that Christ taught and demonstrated with His own life.

A Word of Caution

Every Christian must remember that Christ was *perfect* in His attitudes and actions. He never sinned. Though He was truly man, His love for us was never marred by human weakness. Though He was tempted to be selfish, He never was. Though He was tempted to envy, to be rude, to be proud, to be easily angered, He never allowed these temptations to manifest themselves in unrighteous acts. Though He was "tempted in every way, just as we are," still He was "without sin" (Heb. 4:15).

There is no way then that we as Christians can live totally as Christ lived. Yet, God has made it possible for every believer to become more and more conformed to Christ's image (2 Cor. 3:18). This is God's plan. He's our divine example. And His Spirit working through the Word of God and other members of the body of Christ, is our source of power, encouragement, and enablement. It is indeed possible to imitate Christ, the Supreme Servant, though we will never be like Him in all respects, even in eternity.

Each of us, however, must stop and ask ourselves where we are in the process of becoming a Christlike servant to others. For most of us, no matter where we are in the process, the challenge is great.

My own heart was moved by the story of a Chinese Christian by the name of Lough Fook. Moved with a compassion for the coolies in the South African mines, he sold himself for a term of five years as a coolie slave and was transported to Demerara to carry the Gospel to his countrymen working there. He toiled in the mines with them and preached Jesus while he worked, till he had scores of converts to Christ.

Lough Fook died, but not until he had won to the Saviour nearly 200 disciples who joined the Christian church. Where, we might ask, throughout the centuries do we have an illustration of what Christ did for all mankind when *He* "made Himself nothing, taking the very nature of a servant" (Phil. 2:7). To what extent do you demonstrate the same attitude as Jesus Christ?

Some Personal Questions

1. To what extent do I exemplify Christ's *unselfish* attitudes?
2. To what extent do I exemplify Christ's *humble* spirit?
3. To what extent do I exemplify Christ's supreme *sacrificial* act of love?

11
Servant Examples

After exhorting the Philippians to exemplify Christ's servant attitudes, Paul wrote about two men who are unusual "servant examples"—Timothy and Epaphroditus. The *unselfish, humble,* and *sacrificial* attitudes and actions of these men are clear in their service for the Lord. However, in writing about them, Paul emphasized the ultimate quality of Christ—self-sacrifice. A Christian exhibits this kind of behavior *only* if the other two qualities are present. Unselfishness leads to sacrificial service, and humility causes a Christian to put others first. Timothy and Epaphroditus both characterize this reality.

Timothy

I have no one else like him (Phil. 2:20).

Prologue: WHAT WAS TIMOTHY'S BACKGROUND? Timothy was first exposed to the Gospel on Paul's first missionary journey.

It was in his hometown, Lystra, that Paul had healed a lame man, causing a crowd of people to identify both Paul and Barnabas as Greek gods. Ironically, these people who wanted to bow down and worship these men eventually turned on them in extreme anger. Paul was singled out and dragged out of the city and stoned. Thinking they had killed him, the crowds dispersed. However, we read that "after the disciples had gathered around him, he got up and went back into the city. The next day he and Barnabas left for Derbe" (Acts 14:20). In some miraculous way, God preserved Paul's life and brought instant healing, enabling him to continue his missionary ministry 24 hours later.

Probably standing among these "disciples" who "had gathered around" was a young man named Timothy. He was a product of a mixed marriage. His mother was a very devoted Jew who taught him the Old Testament Scriptures from childhood (2 Tim. 3:14-15). His father was a Gentile (Acts 16:1). It appears that Timothy responded to the Gospel when he first heard it preached on Paul's first visit to his hometown. Little did he realize at that moment as he watched God's miraculous intervention in Paul's life that he would eventually be one of this great apostle's most trusted missionary companions.

On Paul's second journey he returned to Lystra with another missionary named Silas, and he was personally introduced to Timothy. Luke records that "the brothers at Lystra and Iconium spoke well of him [Timothy]" (16:2). Timothy had developed a reputation as a devoted Christian, not only in his hometown, but in surrounding communities. Paul was so impressed with this young man's Christian witness and maturity that he invited Timothy to join him and Silas as a fellow missionary.

As these men traveled together, they eventually came to Philippi, a city in Macedonia, where they planted a strong and dynamic church (16:11-40). Years later when Paul was held captive as a prisoner in Rome, he wrote a letter to this church. It's in this letter that we discover the great "Kenosis passage" we looked at in our last chapter. And it is in this letter that Paul talked openly about Timothy's sacrificial service.

Paul's profile: WHY WAS TIMOTHY AN OUTSTANDING SERVANT EXAMPLE? Paul asked Timothy to visit the Philippian church so he might find out how they were doing. While reporting on this request in the Philippian letter, he made a very significant statement about Timothy. "I have no one else like him, who takes a genuine interest in your welfare," Paul wrote. "For everyone looks out for his own interests, not those of Jesus Christ" (Phil. 2:20-21). Paul then made it clear that this statement was not made on the basis of casual acquaintance. "But you know," he continued, "that Timothy has proved himself, because as a son with his father he has *served* with me in the work of the Gospel" (v. 22).

We're not really sure what Paul actually meant when he said, "I have no one else like him." However, it seems logical from the context that he was making at least two points.

First, Timothy was the only Christian in Rome (excluding Epaphroditus) who cared enough about the Philippian Christians to make the trip to Philippi to see how they were doing. Everyone else seemed to be so involved in their own affairs that they would not take the time or make the effort to assist Paul in this matter. But Timothy, as usual, was willing.

Second, Timothy was a Christian who exemplified the self-sacrificing qualities of Jesus Christ. (Compare 2:4 with 2:20-21.) There's a very significant correlation between what Paul stated earlier in this letter—just before he described Christ's attitudes—and what he wrote about Timothy. "Each of you should look not only to your *own interests*, but also to the *interests of others*," he had written (2:4). And in describing Timothy, he stated, "I have no one else like him, who takes a *genuine interest* in your welfare. For everyone looks out for his *own interests*, not those of Jesus Christ" (vv. 20-21).

Timothy, then, stands out as a unique "servant example" for the Philippian Christians, but also for every 20th-century Christian. The basic decision he made must have been very difficult, but he nevertheless made it because he knew how much Paul wanted to know how these Philippian Christians were doing in their Christian lives.

We can also be sure that he was emotionally torn between leaving Paul alone in prison and traveling to see the Philippians. He knew how much Paul needed his help and encouragement. Ultimately, it must have been Paul's own willingness to sacrifice Timothy's presence that caused this young man to be willing to make the trip.

Remember too this was not an overnight jaunt by jet. It would take weeks to make the trip from Rome to Philippi. But this did not deter Timothy. Furthermore, it was not a new experience. He had "proved himself" many times before as he traveled by Paul's side and "*served* with" him "in the work of the Gospel."

Postscript: WAS TIMOTHY A SUPER-CHRISTIAN? At this juncture you may be tempted to think of Timothy as a super-Christian who had all of the natural qualities that would make him a born leader. Not so! Rather, he had several strikes against him.

First, he was a young man attempting to do a "man-sized" job. Can you imagine having to be Paul's representative? People were no different in those days—they made comparisons. That was a big hurdle for Timothy. Consequently, Paul had to encourage him. "Don't let anyone look down on you because you are young, but set an example for the believers in speech, in life, in love, in faith, and in purity" (1 Tim. 4:12).

Because of his youth and Paul's overpowering shadow, Timothy often became intimidated and threatened. Even in his final letter just before his death, Paul encouraged Timothy in this area of his life. "God did not give us a spirit of timidity, but a spirit of power, of love, and of self-discipline. So," Paul continued, "do not be ashamed to testify about our Lord, or ashamed of me His prisoner" (2 Tim. 1:7-8).

Timothy had yet another handicap. He had stomach problems. Perhaps they were psychosomatic because of his insecurity and fear. Consequently, Paul told him on one occasion to "stop drinking only water, but use a little wine because of your stomach and your frequent illnesses" (1 Tim. 5:23).

Epaphroditus

He almost died for the work of Christ (Phil. 2:30).

Paul next made reference to Epaphroditus. We really know very little about this man, except what is revealed in this paragraph in Paul's letter. But what we learn is indeed impressive. His relationship with Paul must have been a longstanding one since Paul identified him as a "brother," a "fellow worker," and a "fellow soldier" (v. 25a).

We also know the following facts:

- The Philippians had sent Epaphroditus to Rome with a special gift to meet Paul's needs (v. 25b).

- While in Rome, Epaphroditus became ill and almost died (vv. 27, 30).

- This illness was caused when Epaphroditus risked his life to compensate for the help the Philippians could not give Paul (v. 30).

- When the Philippians heard Epaphroditus was ill because of his life-risking experience, they were very concerned (v. 26).

- When Epaphroditus in turn discovered that the Philippian Christians had heard about his illness, he became very distressed, evidently because he did not want to worry them (v. 26).

- Paul was also emotionally disturbed over this whole experience. He was anxious about the Philippians' reactions to Epaphroditus' illness (v.28).

- Paul exhorted the Philippians to be sure to welcome Epaphroditus home in a special way and to honor him for his sacrificial service on behalf of them as well as Paul (v. 29).

From these basic facts about Epaphroditus, we can draw some fairly safe conclusions. This man had a long-term and very meaningful relationship with the Philippians. He was deeply trusted, for they had entrusted him with their sacrificial gift to Paul. And it was "sacrificial" because they couldn't send enough to care for Paul's total needs. In fact, Paul refers in his Corinthian letter to the churches in Macedonia that gave out of their poverty (2 Cor. 8:1-2). The Philippians were no doubt one of these churches.

Epaphroditus, knowing Paul's needs were greater than the gift, evidently did something to make up the difference, risking his life in the process. What this involved, we can only speculate. Perhaps he overtaxed his physical and emotional reserves. But whatever happened, he definitely put others' interests ahead of his own. Paul's needs became more important to him than his own. And the Philippians' concern for Paul motivated Epaphroditus to go beyond the call of duty.

A Call for More Christians Like Timothy and Epaphroditus

What do these "servant examples" teach every 20th-century Christian believer? First, and foremost, we need more Christians who are willing to put others' interests and needs before their own, particularly as they relate to carrying out Christ's work in this world. However, most of us cannot relate to the circumstances surrounding Timothy and Epaphroditus, particularly those of us living in a *free society.* Furthermore, most of us cannot relate to the Philippian Christians and their sacrificial gifts. When we share our material possessions, for example, we share out of *plenty*—comparatively speaking—not *poverty.* Also, few of us have ever had to face the decisions Timothy faced, nor do we confront the challenges of risking our lives to meet another person's needs.

How should we relate to these facts? Should we feel guilty?

- Because we have more freedom than Christians in the first century?
- Because we have more material blessings than New Testament Christians?
- Because we are not called upon to risk our lives for the Gospel of Christ?
- Because we have unparalleled opportunities to better ourselves in every way than most Christians have ever had throughout the centuries?

I don't believe so! This is not what God says in His Word directly nor is He saying it through men like Timothy and Epaphroditus. This is not the issue. Rather, we should thank God for our blessings and enjoy them to the fullest. We may not always have them, and then we'll be able to identify with Paul's statement, "I know what it is to be in need, and I know what it is to have plenty. I have learned the secret of being content in any and every situation, whether well fed or hungry, whether living in plenty or in want. I can do everything through Him who gives me strength" (Phil. 4:12-13).

However, when should a Christian feel guilty? This is a very difficult question to answer. In fact, I'm trying to face that question myself, particularly as a pastor. For example, how much time should I devote to meeting the needs of my own family compared with meeting the needs of the "larger family" of God? How much time should I plan for leisure time when the needs of people are endless? How much effort should I devote to planning for my own future—and more important, my wife's future? Furthermore, what does all of this mean? What do I need to be secure? What does my wife need? How much is "enough"? How much is "too much" in view of the needs that are all around us? When does dependence on the Lord and faith become "presumption" and "irresponsibility"? And, the question that I face particularly as a full-time Christian worker: Am I entitled to the same security as people who are not full-time Christian workers, or is more expected of me automatically because I'm a spiritual leader?

No one can answer these questions for me *specifically.* They are my responsibility to face and answer in the light of God's eternal principles that are set forth in the Word of God. I must work out the *specifics*—and that is not easy.

Biblical Principles and Guidelines

1. No decision should ever contradict the direct teaching of Scripture. We must be careful, however, how we use Scripture. For example, there are statements in Scripture that if taken out of context can lead to some very foolish decisions. For example, Jesus said on one occasion, sell all you have and give to the poor (Mark 10:21). He also said to not worry about tomorrow (Matt. 6:34). And on another occasion He said if someone asks you for your tunic, give him your cloak also (5:40).

To apply these teachings without considering the larger context of Scripture and even the immediate context of what Jesus had in mind can indeed lead to some disastrous decisions. Some Christians use Scriptures out of context to lead them not to consult doctors, not to buy insurance, not to have any savings, etc. The total context of Scripture makes it clear this is *not* what God had in mind.

2. All decisions should first of all be made in the light of eternal values, not earthly values. Again, this does not mean that earthly concerns are not important. It simply means that everything on this earth will pass away and only eternal values will last forever. Jesus said, "But seek first His kingdom and His righteousness, and all these things will be given to you as well" (Matt. 6:33).

3. All decisions should be balanced between faith on the one hand, and common sense and rational thinking on the other hand. It is true that God's Word says, "Trust in the Lord with all your heart and lean not on your own understanding; in all your ways acknowledge Him, and He will make your paths straight" (Prov. 3:5-6). Faith and trust must always take precedence over human wisdom. But to trust God does not mean that we do not use the gift of intelligence that God has given us. God simply warns that we should not "lean" on our own understanding. When we put more confidence in ourselves than we do in God, we will make decisions that are selfish and built around our own interests rather than the interests of the Lord and others.

4. All decisions should be made in the light of Romans 12:1-2. If I offer my body to Christ as a living sacrifice, if I am not conformed any longer to the pattern of this world but rather, I am being transformed into the image of Christ by the renewing of my mind, then God says, I "will be able to test and approve what God's will is—His good, pleasing, and perfect will" (12:2). This is the beginning point in decision-making that is in harmony with the will of God. If I'm conforming my life to the pattern of this world, I will make

decisions that are man-centered rather than God-centered.

5. All decisions should be made after faithful and diligent prayer—"Lord, what do You want *me* to do?" However, if we have not carried out God's specific and revealed will in our lives, this is the place to begin.

Prayer is no magic solution for finding God's will in *specific areas* of our lives if we have not obeyed God in *specific areas* revealed in Scripture.

6. When making significant decisions in areas that are not specifically outlined in Scripture, we need to consult several mature Christians—Christians who know the Word of God and who have dedicated their lives to God.

This does not mean that only full-time pastors and Christian workers are the ones who can answer these questions. In fact, mature Christians who are not involved in vocational Christian work can sometimes be more objective and realistic about life. In actuality, we need both perspectives to arrive at a proper balance.

We need more Christians like Timothy and Epaphroditus—Christians who are willing to put God and others first, no matter what the circumstances. Needless to say, this is a process. No one decision will ever be adequate for all time. Circumstances change. Twenty years from now many of the issues we wrestle with may no longer be relevant. But God's eternal principles will always be relevant in every situation of life. And one of those principles is that we always be servants of God and one another.

12
A Servant's Reward

One day a patient was admitted to Johns Hopkins Hospital. She was a middle-aged lady from a rural area and very ill. Dr. Howard Kelly, the chief surgeon, seeing her condition, spared no effort to help her. After surgery he outlined a program for special care, including a private room and a private nurse.

Finally, the day came when the patient was well enough to go home. Though happy with her recovery, she dreaded getting the bill. It would be enormous! Determined, however, to face reality, she insisted that the nurse bring it immediately. When she received it she began to read the items one by one. Her heart became heavy and when she saw the total cost, she almost had a relapse. But then her eyes caught a glimpse of a brief notation at the bottom of the bill that overwhelmed her.

Her mind quickly went back many years to a summer day

when a young medical student who was selling books to help pay his way through medical school, stopped at her home and asked for a glass of water. A young girl then, she came to the door. When he asked for the water, she offered him a glass of fresh milk instead. He, of course, accepted it and enjoyed it to the full.

Years had passed when she entered Johns Hopkins Hospital. The young man who had stopped at her door many years before had eventually become Dr. Howard Kelly and the chief surgeon at the hospital. And that day the notation on the bottom of her bill simply read: "Paid in full with one glass of milk." And it was signed, "Howard A. Kelly, M.D."

Someday Jesus Christ will say to every one of His children who have faithfully served Him, "Well done, good and faithful servant!" (Matt. 25:21, 23) And, He will not forget one thing we have done to carry out His work on earth. In fact, He will reward us for even a cup of cool water that has been given in His name (10:42). Since Dr. Howard Kelly was a devout Christian as well as an outstanding doctor, he probably was well aware of this statement by Jesus and decided to imitate Christ that day, not only as a servant, but as a rewarder as well.

Eternal Rewards

PAUL'S ANALOGIES. As you study the concept of rewards in the Bible, the emphasis is clearly on "eternal rewards" for faithful servanthood. Paul, particularly, used figures of speech from the realm of athletics to illustrate that Christians will be rewarded for faithful service. Writing to the Corinthians, he referred to a "prize" for winning a race. "Do you know," he asked, "that in a race all the runners run, but only one gets the *prize?*" (1 Cor. 9:24a)

Paul next applied this analogy to the Christian life. "Run in such a way," he exhorted, "as to get the prize" (v. 24b).

In the next verse, Paul went back to the illustration and talked about preparation to run the race. "Everyone who competes in the games goes into strict training. They do it to get a *crown* that will not last" (v. 25a).

I have a daughter who in her college days participated in a couple of marathons. I was quite amazed and proud of her training program. While preparing for the 26-mile race, she would run 6 to 8 miles a day and 20 miles on Saturday—a total of 60 miles a week. And as the day for the race approached, she prepared herself by running, but also through a very special diet. I admired her self-discipline.

In the "Olympic Games," Paul implied, it's great to win gold, silver, and bronze medals. But, he said, these will not last. A Christian, however, trains and participates "to get a crown that will last forever. Therefore," Paul continued, "I do not run like a man running aimlessly; I do not fight like a man beating the air. No, I beat my body and make it my slave so that after I have preached to others, I myself will not be disqualified for the prize" (vv. 25b-27).

Paul was not talking here about receiving eternal life as the prize. He already had eternal life. He was speaking of rewards for faithful servanthood.

Just before Paul was martyred, he wrote to Timothy, "I have fought the good fight, I have finished the race, I have kept the faith. Now there is in store for me the *crown of righteousness,* which the Lord, the righteous Judge, will award to me on that day—and not only to me, but also to all who have longed for His appearing" (2 Tim. 4:7-8).

Again, Paul was referring to something other than eternal life. He was absolutely sure of his salvation. That was given to him by the grace of God. But, because of his faithfulness to the Lord, he looked forward to a special crown, a special reward—a crown of righteousness.

THE TRUE REWARD. When Paul wrote of the "prize" or "the crown," he was speaking symbolically. Eternal rewards for Christians focus on people—people whose lives we have been able to touch in a special way, leading to conversion and/or spiritual growth. This is clearly illustrated in Paul's letters to the Thessalonians.

When Paul and Silas and Timothy came to Thessalonica preaching the Gospel, a number of people responded and put their faith in Jesus Christ (Acts 17:4). In fact, the Christian missionaries were so successful that they created intense jealousy among the Jews, who in turn hired some criminal types to form a mob and to create a riot (v. 5). Things got so intense that Paul and his two missionary companions had to secretly leave the city at night (vv. 10, 14).

Predictably, Paul was very concerned about what might happen to these new Christians they had to leave behind. The persecution would not automatically subside because they had left Thessalonica. When Paul wrote his first letter to these Christians, he let us in on some of his feelings about these events—and in doing so, also gave us his perspective on eternal rewards.

"But, brothers," he wrote, "when we were torn away from you for a short time (in person, not in thought), out of our intense longing we made every effort to see you. For we wanted to come to you—certainly I, Paul, did, again and again—but Satan stopped us" (1 Thes. 2:17-18).

Paul's motivation was his concern for these believers and what happened to them after they had left the city. The apostle then focused clearly on his eternal perspective of rewards. He wrote, "For what is our hope, our joy, or the *crown* in which we will glory in the presence of our Lord Jesus when He comes? Is it not *you?* Indeed, *you* are our glory and joy" (vv. 19-20). In other words, what would make Paul's sacrificial efforts for Christ worthwhile, would be the people he would join in heaven someday who had responded to the Gospel of Christ and who had grown in their Christian experience.

NO REWARDS. The Scriptures are clear that not everyone who goes to heaven will receive rewards that will be given by the Lord for faithful servanthood. Paul made this point clear in his letter to the Corinthians. It is a sobering declaration. He wrote:

> By the grace God has given me, I laid a foundation as an expert builder, and someone else is building on it. But each one should be careful how he builds. For no one can lay any foundation other than the one already laid, which is Jesus Christ. If any man builds on this foundation using gold, silver, costly stones, wood, hay, or straw, his work will be shown for what it is, because the Day will bring it to light. It will be revealed with fire, and the fire will test the quality of each man's work. If what he has built survives, *he will receive his reward.* If it is burned up, *he will suffer loss;* he himself will be saved, but only as one escaping through the flames (1 Cor. 3:10-15).

There will be Christians then who will be saved, but they

will not be rewarded. This is hard to imagine, for God will not overlook even our most feeble efforts. How encouraging to know that even when we fail Him utterly, He will not close the door to heaven. That, of course, is pure grace!

Earthly Rewards

Interestingly, there is a direct correlation in Paul's view of eternal rewards and earthly rewards for serving Christ. He made this point clear in the same Thessalonian letter. Paul's happiness and encouragement were directly related to the response of the people, not only in salvation but in spiritual growth. Note how this is illustrated in his relationship with these Christians.

As Paul reflected on the Thessalonians and what may have transpired in their lives, he became so emotionally distraught that he sent Timothy to "strengthen and encourage" them in their faith so they would not get sidetracked spiritually. "I was afraid," Paul confessed, "that in some way the tempter might have tempted you and our efforts might have been useless" (1 Thes. 3:2, 5).

Timothy returned, however, with a glowing report. These Christians had grown in their faith in spite of the persecution. They had progressed in their love for God and for one another. And Paul reflected his humanness when he expressed his joy that these Thessalonians had "pleasant memories" of their relationship with these missionaries. They longed to see them just as Paul, Silas, and Timothy longed to see them (v. 6). "Therefore, brothers," he wrote, "in all our distress and persecution we were *encouraged* about you because of your faith. For now we *really live,* since you are standing firm in the Lord. How can we thank God enough for you in return for *all the joy* we have in the presence of our God because of you?" (vv. 7-10)

Earthly rewards then, in serving Christ, focus primarily on the spiritual response of people to whom we minister. Yes, there are disappointments. Not all respond. But those who do make it all worthwhile.

The very week I was preparing this material, I had the privilege of speaking at the Annual Pastors Conference at the Moody Bible Institute in Chicago. Each year between 1,200 and 1,500 pastors gather for inspiration, fellowship, and instruction. It's an exciting opportunity to address these men and to attempt to encourage them in their ministries.

However, my most exciting opportunity came when I was invited to speak in a little inner-city church made up primarily of Hispanics. A couple of years ago the pastor attended one of our Church Renewal Conferences in Dallas sponsored by the Center for Church Renewal. There he became exposed to the New Testament principles I've outlined in *Sharpening the Focus of the Church* (Moody Press), which we have attempted to apply in our own ministry. Also, the pastor later purchased our videotapes on the same subject and used them in ministering to these people. Consequently, when I walked into their humble, little sanctuary in downtown Chicago, I was no stranger, though I had never met these people face-to-face.

Their warm response to my ministry that evening was very rewarding. To top it off, following my ministry they took an offering for the Center for Church Renewal and later handed me a check. This tangible evidence of their love and appreciation for our ministry to them was like "icing on the cake."

As I drove back to Moody Bible Institute that evening, my

heart was very encouraged. Here were people, most of whom did not have the economic opportunities of most people in America, coming to Christ, growing in Christ—and sharing what they had to help others. Speaking to hundreds of pastors and sensing their appreciation was indeed exciting. But ministering to that little group of Hispanic Christians who were attempting to apply the New Testament principles we had taught them on videotape was exhilarating. It made the trip worthwhile. I could not help but think of Paul's words to the Thessalonians, "For what is our hope, our joy, or the crown in which we will glory in the presence of our Lord Jesus when He comes? Is it not *you?* Indeed, *you* are our glory and joy" (1 Thes. 2:19-20).

God's Record System

Today we take pride in our computer technology. And indeed, it is an amazing phenomenon. Thousands of pieces of information can be stored on a tiny chip no larger than a fingernail and instantly recalled with the proper equipment.

But God's record system is beyond anything our minds can comprehend. He is omniscient. He never forgets—except in one area. When we come to Christ, our sins are stricken from the record—once and for all. The blood of Jesus Christ keeps on cleansing us from all sin (1 John 1:9).

On the other hand, God's record system for Christians and their service for Him will never be stricken from the record—even a cup of cold water that has been given in His name. Furthermore, I personally believe God's record system goes far beyond *direct* influence on others. It includes continuing influence.

In the world of sales, some people make a lot of money on

the percentage of income that is generated by people who work under them. That is, you might bring someone into a company who works under you and, in turn, you will make a percentage on his total business. And, in some instances, your "recruits" bring in other people and you still make a percentage on the sales that these people generate.

Just so, I believe God's reward system operates on the same principle. When you, as a Christian, touch a person's life for Christ, you will be rewarded. And when that person touches another person's life, you'll share in that reward as well (Phil. 4:17).

When I think of rewards, I often think of D.L. Moody who was led to Christ by a concerned Sunday School teacher. Moody was 17 years old and worked in a shoe store in Boston. One day the teacher came into the store, talked to the young man regarding his need for Christ, and Moody responded to the Gospel.

In 1856 Moody moved to Chicago where he soon became a very successful businessman. It was his personal ambition to become wealthy, and he was well on his way to achieving his goal when in 1860 he decided to give up his business goal and devote his efforts entirely to Christian ministry.

He started a mission school in an old shanty, formerly a saloon, on the north side of the Chicago River in a vice-ridden section called "Little Hell." The growing Sunday School soon moved to a large hall over the North Market. Moody encouraged his converts to attend the church of their choice, but they, in turn, encouraged him to start his own. Consequently, the Illinois Street Church was founded and after his death it was called Moody Church. Moody served as the first pastor.

Eventually, Moody became a traveling evangelist. Under his ministry thousands came to Christ. Thousands more were challenged to lead others to Christ.

Later, D.L. Moody started a training school which, after his death, was called Moody Bible Institute. Over the years, thousands of people have been prepared there for various kinds of Christian ministry. Of all the thousands of evangelical missionaries around the world, it is estimated that at least 10 percent have studied at Moody Bible Institute.

But Moody Bible Institute became more than a school. Today it has a complex of Christian radio stations throughout the United States. Their goal is to entirely blanket every community by means of satellite communications.

Moody Institute of Science films have been shown around the world and translated into numerous languages. Moody Press books are read in every part of the world. *Moody Monthly* magazine goes into thousands of homes.

As I think of all of this, my mind goes back to a Sunday School teacher in Boston, Massachusetts—a man whose name is known, but very few can ever recall. It was his concern for D.L. Moody that eventuated in what I've just described—and much more. It's my personal opinion that when D.L. Moody stands before the Judgment Seat of Christ to be rewarded for his servant efforts, standing beside him will be a Sunday School teacher, sharing in the glory and joy of all that has transpired and will continue to transpire until Jesus comes again. With Paul they will both be saying, "For what is our hope, our joy, or *the crown* in which we will glory in the presence of our Lord Jesus when He comes? Is it not *you?*" (1 Thes. 2:19) And as D.L. Moody and that "unknown" Sunday School teacher view the thousands of people surrounding God's throne, they will say, "Indeed, you are our glory and joy" (v. 20).

God's Pay

Who does God's work will get God's pay,
However long may seem the day,
However weary be the way;
Though powers and princes thunder "Nay,"
Who does God's work will get God's pay.

He does not pay as others pay,
In gold or land or raiment gay;
In goods that vanish and decay;
But God in wisdom knows a way;
And that is sure, let come what may,
Who does God's work will get God's pay.

Author unknown

Other books in the "One Another" series include:

Building Up One Another

This first book in the series discusses 12 specific "one another" commands of the New Testament and shows how every believer is to take part in building up others. (6-2744)

Loving One Another

This book focuses on evangelism that begins in love. It tells you how to find greater unity and fruitfulness, in your life and in your church. (6-2786)

Encouraging One Another

Gene Getz says, "Both biblically and pragmatically I've discovered that there is a great need for Christians to encourage one another." Drawing on the "encouragement" models of Barnabas and Paul, Dr. Getz tells how you can learn to be an encourager. (6-2256)

PRAYING FOR ONE ANOTHER

Praying for One Another traces the activities and growth of the church in Acts, showing how corporate or "body" praying can become a key to releasing God's power. (6-2351)